DELIGHTFUL THAI COOKING

Design and illustrations by Martine Richards Fabrizio
Typesetting and production by
Technigraphic Systems, Inc., Edmonds, Washington
Editor - Donald R. Bissonnette
Printing by Publishers Press - Salt Lake City, Utah
Cover Photo by Chris Sollart, Technigraphic Systems, Inc.

Published by **Ambrosia Publications**

DELIGHTFUL THAI COOKING

by Eng Tie Ang

Published by:

AMBROSIA PUBLICATIONS

Seattle, Washington

AMBROSIA PUBLICATION
P.O. Box 30818
Seattle, WA 98103
Phone (206) 789-3693
Fax   (206) 789-3693

Printed in the United States of America
First Edition
First Printing - October 1990
Second Printing - March 1991
Third Printing - November 1991
Fourth Printing - March 1993
Fifth Printing - October 1994

ISBN: 0-9627810-4-5

Library of Congress Catalog Number: 90-84825

4

Dedicated to Ang Bun Pit and Kang Siu Tjen, my father and mother, for all that they taught me and for all that I am.

ON THE COVER

1. Chicken Satay, p. 30

2. Satay Peanut Sauce, p. 15

3. Cucumber Sauce, p. 16

4. Mixed Vegetable Salad, p. 49

5. Stir-Fried Noodles, p. 102

6. Steamed Rice

7. Sauted Shrimp with Lemon Grass, p. 71

TABLE OF CONTENTS

Acknowledgements
Introduction

CHAPTER ONE..13
Curry Pastes and Sauces

CHAPTER TWO..23
Appetizers and Snacks

CHAPTER THREE..31
Soups

CHAPTER FOUR...41
Salads

CHAPTER FIVE..53
Vegetables

CHAPTER SIX...63
Seafood

CHAPTER SEVEN..77
Meat and Poultry

CHAPTER EIGHT..97
Rice and Noodles

CHAPTER NINE..105
Desserts

Appendix...113
Diagrams
Essential Ingredients
Glossary
Markets for Thai Ingredients
Index..126
Ordering Information...132

ACKNOWLEDGEMENTS

   I would like to thank many people for their help, support and encouragement in putting this book together . First, my mother, Kang Siu Tjen, who began teaching me how to cook when I was five years old and who for over thirty years has tasted and critiqued my food and encouraged me to learn both traditional and modern recipes. Second, my husband, Donald R. Bissonnette, for his writing and editing help, encouragement to continue, and help with the kids while I was working on the book. For their help in typing and organizing the material, I thank Marte Hugo Gutierrez, Maria de Jesus Gutierrez, and Babu Parayil. For her help with the transliteration of Thai words and suggestions on recipes to include, I am grateful to Mrs. Lamoon Suwanna Cox. For their editing and proofreading help, Roger Bourret, Sara Baldwin and Debbie Turner were of great value and assistance. Kelli Keaton Ambrosi of Technigraphic Systems, Inc., was invaluable in patiently helping me get this printed and published. I sincerely thank Mr. Ralph Gene Waters for his constant encouragement, faith in me, and technical assistance. For their generously allowing me to use various items for the cover photo, I would like to thank Gloria Gunn of Tilden Gift Shop in Seattle for the beautiful dishes and baskets, Nature's Elegance of Seattle for the orchids, and Jennifer Johnson of the Siam Gallery in Seattle for the very beautiful Thai fabrics. And finally, I wish to thank all my cooking class students and friends for their encouragement to undertake this project in the first place. To all of the above, I offer my sincere thanks and gratitude.

straw
mushrooms

mint

green
papaya

INTRODUCTION

Thai cooking is an exquisitely different and distinctive Asian cuisine which has been influenced by and taken from most notably both Chinese and Indian cuisines. Its stir-fry dishes have their roots in China; its curries in India. In fact, the Thai people originally migrated south from China's Yunan province in the 13th century. The Pad Pak Naam Mun Hoy (Broccoli in Oyster Sauce) is undoubtedly Chinese in origin. Later, Indian traders brought with them their curries which the Thai quickly modified, changing them to distinctively Thai dishes. Chicken Masaman Curry is an excellent example of this. Thus, Thai food is a synthesis of ideas and tastes, resulting in a cuisine which is unique and unsurpassed in its mouth-watering dishes.

In Thailand, as in all of South East Asia, food preparation is an art form. The taste of a dish is of utmost importance. However, its preparation and presentation are equally important. Food is more than something just to be eaten: it is also to be savored on all sensory levels. It must have exquisite taste. It must be at the same time fragrant and pungent. Its texture must be both creamy soft and crunchy. And it must present a pleasing picture when served. An array of colors and shapes is essential to a Thai meal. Garnishings are of great importance. A meal is enjoyed by the mouth, nose and eyes. It is a rhapsody of flavor, aroma, and vision.

Now to talk about the tastes of Thai food. Immediately, hot comes to mind, chili hot to be exact. Certainly authentic Thai food comes with its share of heat, but that is not all there is to Thai food. Anyone can add hot chilies to food to make it hot. Thai food is different. It is at once chili-hot, sweet, sour, salty and bitter. A complete meal combines all these tastes. Subtle changes take place within the mouth when an authentic Thai meal is eaten. The diner becomes wonderfully aware of all the distinct flavor combinations simultaneously being recognized by the tongue. It's a superb dining experience. The chilies have their role in the cuisine. They sharpen the tongue to become more aware of the other flavors. They enhance the effect of all the other spices and herbs. That is their role. But they are just part of the blend of tastes, part of the balance of herbs, spices and sauces that is Thai cooking.

11

The recipes in this book have been carefully selected for their genuine and unique authenticity and practicality for use in a Western kitchen. None of them should take much more than an hour to complete. This is especially true once the cook has prepared a supply of the pastes which are used in various recipes and which keep quite a long time when refrigerated. Thai cooking is basically fast cooking. Once one has the supplies, it's simply a matter of putting them together. Like anything else, it's a matter of practice and familiarization: the more one does it, the easier it becomes. Try some of these recipes and prove me right. You will be happy you did.

Speaking of supplies, they are becoming more and more available throughout the U.S., especially in all big cities. Most supermarkets in fact have Asian sections in which most herbs and spices can be found. Cities with sizeable Oriental communities have most of these ingredients available in their local grocery stores.

You will have no difficulty in regard to finding the necessary utensils and apparatus for Thai cooking. Contrary to what one might think, Thai cooking does not require sophisticated equipment. Basically, a food processor or blender is used to make pastes and sauces; a mortar and pestle are used for pounding and grinding small portions of herbs and spices; and a wok definitely makes the stir-frying and deep-frying jobs easier. That's it. If you have the above, you are ready to cook Thai food.

Finally, do not be afraid to modify any of these recipes. If a recipe calls for four hot chilies cut lengthwise and you know that you or others eating the food could not possibly handle that much heat, do not be deterred from preparing the dish. Simply cut down on the chilies. It's no sin. It would certainly never bother a Thai person to alter a recipe to suit an occasion. It should not bother you, either. Also, feel free to modify anything else according to your tastes. That is the way of Thai cooking. Experiment and refine until you have it as you want it. Be adventure-some. That is the key to good Thai cooking. Enjoy!

CHAPTER ONE

CURRY PASTES & SAUCES

galangal, laos root or kha

lemon grass

coriander or cilantro

CHAPTER ONE

CURRY PASTES & SAUCES

RED CHILI SAUCE, *(Nam Prik Dang)* 15

SATAY PEANUT SAUCE, *(Nam Chim Satay)* 15

CUCUMBER SAUCE, *(Nam Chim Taeng Kwa)* 16

PLUM SAUCE, *(Nam Chim Gim Boi)* 16

SWEET AND SOUR SAUCE, *(Nam Chim Priew Waan)* 17

SWEET AND SOUR FISH SAUCE, *(Nam Pla Prig)* 17

CHILI SAUCE WITH TAMARIND, *(Nam Prik Som Mak Kam)* 18

GROUND TOASTED RICE, *(Khao Cua)* 18

MASAMAN CURRY PASTE, *(Nam Prik Gang Masaman)* 19

GREEN CURRY PASTE, *(Nam Prik Kang Khiaw-waan)* 20

RED CURRY PASTE, *(Nam Prik Gang Pet Dang)* 21

YELLOW CURRY PASTE, *(Nam Prik Gang Lugang)* 22

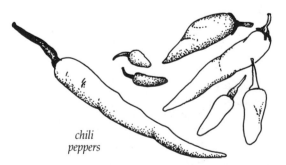

chili peppers

Red Chili Sauce
(Nam Prik Dang)

20 fresh red chilies, chopped

4 cloves garlic, crushed

2 tablespoons brown sugar or palm sugar

2 tablespoons fish sauce (Nam Pla)

1/4 cup fresh lime juice or tamarind liquid

In a blender, grind all the ingredients to a smooth sauce. Put in a tightly closed jar and refrigerate. **Makes 1/2 cup.**

Satay Peanut Sauce
(Nam Chim Satay)

3 cloves garlic, crushed

2 tablespoons vegetable oil

1 cup water

2 fresh hot red chilies, finely chopped

2 tablespoons fresh lime juice

1 teaspoon salt

2 tablespoons brown sugar

1/2 teaspoon shrimp paste (Kapi)

1 cup smooth or crunchy peanut butter

1 can coconut milk (14 fl. oz.)

In a small pan, fry the garlic in the oil until golden brown. Add the water, chilies, lime juice, salt, brown sugar, shrimp paste, peanut butter, and coconut milk and stir until well-blended. Simmer the sauce for about 10 minutes, stirring frequently. To be used with chicken, beef or pork satays. **Makes 3 cups.**

CUCUMBER SAUCE
(Nam Chim Taeng Kwa)

1/2 cup rice vinegar

1/4 cup water

1/2 cup white sugar

1 teaspoon salt

1 cup cucumber, peeled
  and thinly sliced

1/2 teaspoon red cayenne
  powder

In a medium saucepan (2 quart), combine vinegar, water, sugar and salt and bring to a boil over high heat. Let cool. Pour sauce over cucumber before serving. Garnish on top with cayenne powder. Serve with satay. **Makes 1-1/4 cups.**

PLUM SAUCE
(Nam Chim Gim Boi)

6 dried plums, pitted,
  finely chopped

3/4 cup rice vinegar

1/2 cup water

1 cup white sugar

2 teaspoons Red Chili
  Sauce (See page 15.)

1 teaspoon salt

In a blender, grind all the ingredients into a smooth sauce. In a saucepan, cook the sauce over medium-heat until the sauce thickens. Cool and refrigerate up to 2 months. Serve at room temperature. **Makes 1-3/4 cups.**

Sweet and Sour Sauce
(Nam Chim Priew Waan)

1 cup water

1/2 cup sugar

1/4 cup rice vinegar

1/2 teaspoon dried hot red chili pepper, crushed

1 teaspoon salt

2 tablespoons ketchup

2 tablespoons cornstarch, mixed with 4 tablespoons water

Boil the water in a small pot, then lower the heat and add the sugar, vinegar, crushed red chili, salt and ketchup. Gradually add cornstarch, stirring until it becomes loosely thickened. **Makes 1-3/4 cups.**

Sweet and Sour Fish Sauce
(Nam Pla Prig)

4 cloves garlic, finely chopped

1 tablespoon hot red chili or cayenne pepper flakes, crushed

6 tablespoons fresh lime juice

1/4 cup fish sauce, (Nam Pla)

1/2 cup white sugar

1 cup warm water

Combine all the ingredients in a small bowl. Stir well and serve at room temperature. **Makes 1-3/4 cups.**

CHILI SAUCE WITH TAMARIND
(Nam Prik Som Mak Kam)

2 tablespoons dried shrimp, ground in a mortar

5 dried red chilies, crushed

6 cloves garlic, crushed

1 teaspoon shrimp paste (Kapi)

1 cup fish sauce (Nam Pla)

2 tablespoons palm sugar or brown sugar

2 tablespoons tamarind, dissolved in 8 tablespoons hot water

In a small bowl, mix thoroughly the ground dried shrimp, red chilies, garlic, shrimp paste, fish sauce, palm sugar, and tamarind liquid. (Discard the pulp.) Serve with Stuffed Deep-Fried Chicken Wings. **Makes 1-1/2 cups.**

GROUND TOASTED RICE
(Khao Cua)

1/2 cup short grain rice (uncooked)

Place rice in a dry wok and heat over moderate heat, stirring frequently to keep it from burning and to allow it to develop a uniform, deep golden color (approximately 2 to 3 minutes). Then remove it from the heat and let it cool to room temperature. Grind into a fine powder in a blender or a spice or coffee grinder. **Makes 1/4 cup.**

MASAMAN CURRY PASTE
(Nam Prik Gang Masaman)

10 dried red chilies, soaked, chopped

2 teaspoons ground coriander

1 teaspoon ground cumin

1 teaspoon ground nutmeg

5 cardamom pods (or 1/2 teaspoon powdered)

1 teaspoon ground cinnamon

1/2 teaspoon ground cloves

6 cloves garlic, crushed

1 large red onion, chopped

1 teaspoon ground black pepper

1 teaspoon shrimp paste (Kapi)

2 teaspoons salt

4 tablespoons finely chopped fresh lemon grass (or 2 tablespoons powdered)

1 one-inch piece dried galangal (Kha) (or 1 teaspoon powdered)

4 bay leaves

In a blender (except for the bay leaves) grind all the ingredients into a paste. When using dried galangal, add it and the bay leaves directly when making curried chicken or beef. **Makes 1/2 cup.**

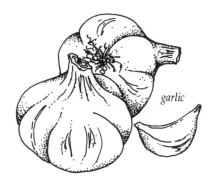

garlic

GREEN CURRY PASTE
(Nam Prik Kang Khiaw-waan)

10 fresh green chilies,
  chopped

4 cloves garlic, crushed

1 onion, chopped

1/2 cup fresh coriander,
  chopped

2 teaspoons salt

2 teaspoons ground
  coriander

1 teaspoon ground cumin

1 teaspoon shrimp paste
  (Kapi)

1 teaspoon ground, or 1
  inch dried, galangal
  (Kha)

1 teaspoon ground, or 1
  stalk fresh, lemon grass

In a blender, grind all the ingredients into a paste. When using dried galangal or fresh lemon grass, add both ingredients directly when cooking the curry. When using dried galangal, soak it in 4 tablespoons of hot water and use soaking water with galangal to give the curry a strong flavor. **Makes 1/2 cup.**

Red Curry Paste
(Nam Prik Gang Pet Dang)

10 dried red chilies, soaked
  and chopped

1 red onion, chopped

3 cloves garlic, crushed

2 teaspoons ground
  coriander

1 teaspoon ground cumin

1 teaspoon shrimp paste
  (Kapi)

2 teaspoons salt

1 teaspoon ground, or 1
  stalk fresh, lemon grass

1 teaspoon ground, or 1
  inch dried, galangal
  (Kha)

In a blender, grind all the ingredients into a paste. When using dried galangal and fresh lemon grass, add both ingredients directly when cooking the curry. When using dried galangal, soak it in 4 tablespoons of hot water and use soaking water with galangal to give the curry a strong flavor. **Makes 1/2 cup.**

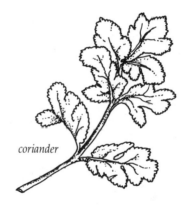

coriander

21

YELLOW CURRY PASTE
(Nam Prik Gang Lugang)

10 dried red chilies, soaked, chopped

1 red onion, chopped

3 cloves garlic, crushed

2 tablespoons fresh coriander, chopped

2 tablespoons chopped fresh lemon grass, (or 1 tablespoon powdered)

1 tablespoon ground cumin

2 tablespoons ground coriander

2 teapoons ground turmeric

2 teaspoons salt

In a blender, grind all the ingredients into a smooth paste. Used for vegetable, seafood, beef, chicken and pork dishes. **Makes 1/2 cup.**

CHAPTER TWO

APPETIZERS & SNACKS

shallots

sweet
basil

garlic

CHAPTER TWO

APPETIZERS & SNACKS

GALLOPING HORSES, *(Ma Hoa)* 25

STUFFED TOFU WITH GROUND PORK, *(Tao Hoo Yod Sai)* 26

STUFFED DEEP-FRIED CHICKEN WINGS, *(Peek Gai Yod Sai)* 27

THAI SPRING ROLLS, *(Pa Pia)* 28

DEEP-FRIED FISH CAKES, *(Tod Mun Pla)* 29

THAI SATAY, *(Satay Thai)* 30

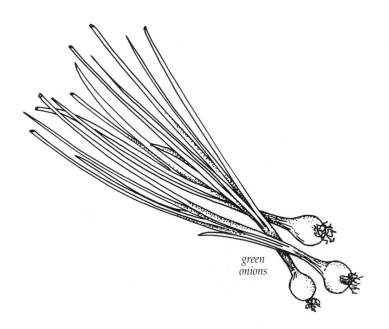

green onions

GALLOPING HORSES
(Ma Hoa)

2 tablespoons vegetable oil

4 tablespoons red onion,
finely chopped

2 tablespoons finely
chopped garlic

1 lb minced lean pork

2 tablespoons fish sauce
(Nam Pla)

1/2 teaspoon ground white
pepper

1 tablespoon white sugar

1 cup ground, roasted,
unsalted peanuts

1 medium to large fresh
pineapple, peeled and
sliced with the hard center
removed; or 1 head leaf
lettuce and two tangerines,
divided into wedges.

2 hot red chilies, finely
chopped

1/2 cup fresh coriander
leaves, chopped

Heat the oil in a frying pan over medium heat and saute the onion and garlic for 1 minute. Add the pork, fish sauce, pepper, and sugar, stirring well and cooking over a moderate heat for 10 minutes. Stir in the peanuts and remove from the heat. Arrange the pineapple slices (or lettuce leaves and tangerine wedges) on individual plates and spoon a portion of the pork mixture into each. Garnish with a few chili peppers and a sprinkling of coriander leaves. **Serves 4-6.**

STUFFED TOFU WITH GROUND PORK
(Tao Hoo Yod Sai)

1 pkg. tofu (14.2 oz.)

1/4 lb ground lean pork

3 cloves garlic, crushed

2 tablespoons green onion, finely chopped

2 tablespoons fresh coriander, chopped

1/2 teaspoon salt

1 teaspoon ground white pepper

1 tablespoon cornstarch

1 egg, beaten

2 cups vegetable oil for deep-frying

Cut tofu into 1-inch cubes. Scoop out the center of each cube. Set aside the outer tofu shells. In a medium bowl, mix the scooped out tofu, pork, garlic, green onion, coriander, salt, pepper, cornstarch, and egg. Stuff the tofu cubes with the mixture. Heat oil in a wok over medium heat and deep-fry the stuffed tofu until golden brown. Drain on paper towels. Serve with Sweet and Sour Sauce. (See page 17.) **Serves 4.**

STUFFED DEEP-FRIED CHICKEN WINGS
(Peek Gai Yod Sai)

2 lbs chicken wings,
  deboned

1 pkg. cellophane noodles,
  soaked in hot water for 3
  minutes, drained

1 lb medium shrimp,
  shelled and deveined
  (See diagram, page 116.)

1 carrot, shredded

1/8 cup water chestnuts,
  finely chopped

1/4 cup green onion, finely
  chopped

4 cloves garlic, crushed

2 tablespoons fish sauce
  (Nam Pla)

1 tablespoon fresh
  coriander, finely
  chopped

1 teaspoon ground white
  pepper

1 cup rice flour

3 cups vegetable oil for
  deep-frying

Debone chicken wings. (See diagram, page 114.) Set meat aside. Cut the cellophane noodles into 1-inch lengths. In a blender or food processor, blend the chicken and shrimp. In a bowl, combine the mixture with carrot, water chestnuts, green onion, garlic, fish sauce, coriander, white pepper, and cellophane noodles. Mix thoroughly. Stuff the wings with mixture. Coat the wings with rice flour and deep-fry in a wok over medium heat for about 3 minutes on each side or until golden brown. Serve with Chili Sauce with Tamarind. (See page 18.) **Serves 6-8.**

THAI SPRING ROLLS
(Pa Pia)

4 tablespoons vegetable oil

4 cloves garlic, chopped

4 tablespoons fresh
coriander, chopped

1 can crab meat (6 1/2 oz.),
drained

1 lb ground pork

2 eggs, beaten

1 cup carrots, shredded

1 small onion, finely
chopped

2 tablespoons fish sauce
(Nam Pla)

1 teaspoon ground white
pepper

2 teaspoons white sugar

1 teaspoon salt

1 3-1/2 oz. pkg. cellophane
noodles, soaked in warm
water for 5 minutes,
drained, cut into 2-inch
lengths

1 pkg. spring roll wrappers
(25 square wrappers)

1 egg yolk mixed with 1
tablespoon water (for
sealing Spring Rolls)

2-3 cups vegetable oil for
deep-frying

In a small frying pan with oil, stir-fry over medium heat the garlic and coriander for two seconds. Pour the mixture in a large bowl and mix thoroughly with the crab, pork, eggs, carrots, onions, fish sauce, pepper, sugar, salt and cellophane noodles. Separate the spring roll wrappers. Place a wrapper with one pointed edge toward you. On each corner put a little of the egg mixture to seal the edges of the spring roll. Put two tablespoons of the mixture one-third of the way from the closest edge. Fold the closest edge over the filling, then fold over the right and left edges, then roll. (See diagram, page 113.) Continue making the egg rolls until all are ready. Place the finished rolls, seam side down, on a large flat serving platter until ready to fry. Do not let them touch each other; otherwise, they will stick together. In a large wok, heat the oil over medium-high heat for 1 minute. Carefully place 3 rolls at a time in oil and deep-fry slowly until both sides are golden brown, about 3 minutes each side. Serve with Sweet and Sour Sauce (See page 17.) or Cucumber Sauce (See page 16.). **Serves 6-8.**

DEEP-FRIED FISH CAKES
(Tod Mun Pla)

1 lb fillet of flounder or sole, finely minced

1 teaspoon salt

1/4 cup Red Curry Paste (See page 21.)

1 egg white

1/2 cup raw green beans, finely chopped

1 tablespoon fish sauce (Nam Pla)

2 kaffir lime leaves, finely chopped

2 tablespoons vegetable oil

2 cups vegetable oil for deep-frying

In a bowl, thoroughly mix the minced fish, salt, curry paste, egg white, green beans, fish sauce, and kaffir lime leaves. To make the fish cake patties, first put oil on the palms of both hands. Then shape the fish paste into balls. Next, flatten to form a 2 inch patty. Be sure to put oil onto your palms before making each patty. After heating the oil to medium hot in a wok, deep-fry the fish patties until golden brown on both sides. Dry on paper towels. Serve with Cucumber Salad (See page 51.).
Serves 4-6.

kaffir lime leaves

THAI SATAY
(Satay Thai)

2 lbs tenderloin pork,
   thinly sliced or in 1-inch
   cubes

6 cloves garlic, crushed

1 tablespoon ground
   coriander

1 tablespoon ground cumin

1 tablespoon ground
   turmeric

1 teaspoon ground white
   pepper

1 tablespoon brown sugar

1 teaspoon salt

1/2 cup coconut milk

bamboo skewers

In a bowl, mix thorougly the sliced pork, garlic, coriander, cumin, turmeric, pepper, sugar, salt, and coconut milk. Marinate the pork for at least 1 hour or overnight, refrigerated. Put 4 pieces of pork on each skewer and broil over a hot charcoal fire until cooked through-out, or in the oven for 3 minutes on each side. Serve with Cucumber Sauce (See page 16.) or Peanut Sauce (See page 15.). The same mixture is used for beef and chicken. **Serves 4-6.**

CHAPTER THREE

SOUPS

kaffir lime
leaves

straw
mushrooms

coconut

CHAPTER THREE

SOUPS

CHICKEN IN COCONUT SOUP, *(Tom Kah Gai)* 33

CHICKEN RICE SOUP, *(Khao Tom Gai)* 34

CURRIED PRAWN SOUP, *(Gaeng Som Goong)* 35

HOT AND SOUR PRAWN SOUP, *(Tom Yum Goong)* 36

HOT AND SOUR SEAFOOD SOUP, *(Tom Yum Talay)* 37

SWEET & SOUR FISH SOUP, *(Tom Som Pla)* 38

SPICY BEEF SOUP, *(Tom Yum Nuea)* 39

COCONUT PUMPKIN SOUP, *(Gaeng Liang Fak Thong)* 40

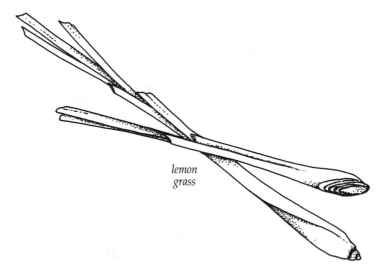

lemon grass

CHICKEN IN COCONUT SOUP
(Tom Kah Gai)

2 tablespoons vegetable oil

4 cloves garlic, crushed

4 tablespoons green onion, finely chopped

1 stalk lemon grass, cut into 2-inch lengths

1 teaspoon ground black pepper

1 teaspoon Red Curry Paste (See page 21.)

2 green chilies, finely chopped

4 kaffir lime leaves

1 one-inch piece dried galangal (Kha)

3 cups water

1 lb chicken breast, finely sliced

2 tablespoons cornstarch

1 can coconut milk (14 fl. oz.)

1 can straw mushrooms (15 oz.), drained

1/4 cup fish sauce (Nam Pla)

1/8 cup fresh lime juice

6 tablespoons fresh coriander, chopped

In a medium-sized pot with oil, stir-fry the garlic, green onion, lemon grass, pepper, curry paste, green chilies, kaffir leaves, and galangal for 2 minutes. Add the water and bring to a boil. Coat the sliced chicken with cornstarch and add it to the soup. Cook for 4 minutes. Add the coconut milk, mushrooms, fish sauce, lime juice and simmer for 2 more minutes. Garnish with fresh coriander. **Serves 4-6.**

CHICKEN RICE SOUP
(Khao Tom Gai)

1 cup short grain rice,
   washed and drained

8 cups water

1 teaspoon salt

2 lbs boneless chicken
   breast, thinly sliced

2 tablespoons fresh lime
   juice, mixed with
   1 teaspoon salt

4 tablespoons vegetable oil

1/2 cup yellow onion,
   finely chopped

3 cloves garlic, crushed

1 teaspoon ground white
   pepper

1/4 cup green onion, finely
   chopped

1/4 cup celery leaves, finely
   chopped

1/4 cup fresh coriander
   leaves

In a medium-sized pot over low heat, simmer the rice, water and salt for about 1 hour or until the rice is soft. Marinate chicken in lime juice with salt for 5 minutes. In a frying pan, heat oil and saute onion and garlic until golden brown. Add the white pepper and marinated chicken. Stir for 10 minutes. In small bowls, put 1 cup heated rice broth and sprinkle with chicken, green onion, celery, and fresh coriander leaves. **Serves 4-6.**

CURRIED PRAWN SOUP
(Gaeng Som Goong)

7 cups water

1 small green papaya,
seeded, thinly sliced

1 can baby corn (15 oz.)

4 fresh hot red chilies,
thinly sliced

4 cloves garlic, crushed

1 one-inch piece dried
galangal (Kha)

1 teaspoon ground
turmeric

1 stalk fresh lemon grass,
cut into 2-inch lengths

4 kaffir lime leaves

1 teaspoon shrimp paste
(Kapi)

2 tablespoons brown sugar

1/4 cup fish sauce
(Nam Pla)

1 tablespoon tamarind
liquid or fresh lime juice

1 lb medium-sized prawns,
shelled, deveined

4 tablespoons green onion,
chopped

Bring the water to a boil. Add the papaya, baby corn, red chilies, garlic, galangal, turmeric, lemon grass, lime leaves, shrimp paste, brown sugar, fish sauce and tamarind liquid. Simmer for 2 minutes and add the prawns and boil for 3 more minutes. Garnish with green onion. **Serves 4-6.**

*chili
peppers*

Hot and Sour Prawn Soup
(Tom Yum Goong)

4 tablespoons vegetable oil

4 cloves garlic, crushed

1 small red onion, finely chopped

7 cups water

1 teaspoon ground black pepper

1 stalk lemon grass, cut into 2-inch lengths

1 one-inch piece dried galangal (Kha)

2 fresh red chilies, thinly sliced

2 fresh green chilies, thinly sliced

4 kaffir lime leaves

1 lb medium-sized prawns, shelled, deveined

6 tablespoons fish sauce (Nam Pla)

2 tablespoons fresh lime juice

4 tablespoons fresh coriander, chopped

Heat the oil in a pot and stir-fry the garlic and onion until light brown. Add the water and bring to a boil. Add the black pepper, lemon grass , galangal, red chilies , green chilies and lime leaves. Boil for 2 minutes and add the prawns, fish sauce and lime juice. Allow to simmer for 3 more minutes and garnish with fresh coriander. **Serves 4-6.**

HOT AND SOUR SEAFOOD SOUP
(Tom Yum Talay)

2 tablespoons vegetable oil

2 cloves garlic, crushed

7 cups water

6 tablespoons fish sauce (Nam Pla)

6 kaffir lime leaves

2 stalks lemon grass, cut into 2-inch lengths

1 lb fresh, medium-sized shrimp, shelled and deveined (See diagram, page 116.)

1 lb sea bass, cut into 1-inch squares

1 can dungeness crabmeat (6 oz.)

1 can baby corn (15 oz.)

1 can straw mushrooms (15 oz.)

4 tablespoons fresh lime juice

2 fresh red chilies, sliced

2 tablespoons green onions, chopped

4 tablespoons fresh coriander leaves

In a large pot with oil, stir-fry the garlic until golden brown. Add the water and bring to a boil. Add the fish sauce, kaffir lime leaves, lemon grass, shrimp, and sea bass and cook for 3 minutes. Add the crabmeat, baby corn, straw mushrooms and lime juice and simmer for 2 more minutes. Garnish with red chilies, green onion, and fresh coriander leaves. **Serves 4-6.**

Sweet & Sour Fish Soup
(Tom Som Pla)

4 tablespoons vegetable oil

1/2 inch piece fresh ginger, thinly sliced

3 cloves garlic, crushed

1 teaspoon shrimp paste (Kapi)

1/2 teaspoon ground turmeric

1 teaspoon ground black pepper

1 teaspoon salt

7 cups water

1 tablespoon tamarind, dissolved in 4 tablespoons of hot water; or juice of 1 lime

2 tablespoons brown sugar

1/2 lb sea bass, cut into 1-inch squares

1/4 cup green cabbage, cut into 1-inch squares

1/2 cup fresh green beans, cut into 1-inch lengths

4 tablespoons fresh coriander, chopped

4 tablespoons green onion, chopped

In a pot with oil, stir-fry the ginger, garlic, shrimp paste, turmeric, pepper, and salt for 1 minute. Add the water, tamarind liquid, and brown sugar. Bring to a boil and add the seabass, cabbage, green beans and cook for 3 minutes. Garnish with fresh coriander and green onion. Serve hot. **Serves 4-6.**

Spicy Beef Soup
(Tom Yum Nuea)

4 tablespoons vegetable oil

4 cloves garlic, crushed

1 small red onion, finely chopped

1 lb round steak, thinly sliced

6 cups water

8 dried red chilies, thinly sliced

4 tablespoons fish sauce (Nam Pla)

1 tablespoon brown sugar

1/8 cup fresh lime juice

1 stalk fresh lemon grass, cut into 2-inch lengths

1 one-inch piece dried galangal (Kha)

4 tablespoons green onion, finely chopped

4 tablespoons fresh coriander, chopped

In a medium-sized pot, heat the oil and stir-fry the garlic and onion until golden brown. Add the sliced beef and stir for 1 minute. Add the water, red chilies, fish sauce, sugar, lime juice, lemon grass, and galangal. Simmer for 20 minutes or until the beef is tender. Garnish with green onion and fresh coriander. **Serves 4-6.**

galangal, laos root or kha

COCONUT PUMPKIN SOUP
(Gaeng Liang Fak Thong)

2 tablespoons vegetable oil

1/4 cup onion , finely chopped

1/4 cup dried shrimp, soaked, finely chopped

2 fresh red chilies, thinly sliced

2 fresh green chilies, thinly sliced

1 teaspoon shrimp paste (Kapi)

6 cups water

2 cups fresh pumpkin, cut into 1-inch squares

1 can coconut milk (14 fl. oz.)

1 teaspoon salt

2 tablespoons fresh lemon juice

4 tablespoons fresh coriander, chopped

8 fresh sweet basil leaves

In a medium-sized pot with oil, stir-fry the onion until golden brown. Add the dried shrimp, red chilies, green chilies, and shrimp paste. Fry for 1 minute. Add the water and bring to a boil. Then, add the pumpkin, reduce heat and simmer for 10 minutes. Add coconut milk and salt. Bring back to the boil and continue to cook until the pumpkin is tender. Garnish with lemon juice, coriander and basil leaves. Serve hot. **Serves 4-6.**

CHAPTER FOUR

SALADS

lemon
grass

kaffir lime
leaves

green
papaya

CHAPTER FOUR

SALADS

SPICY PRAWN SALAD, *(Yaam Goong)* 43

DRIED SHRIMP SALAD, *(Larb)* 44

THAI SQUID SALAD, *(Yaam Pla Mouk)* 45

THAI BEEF SALAD, *(Yaam Nuea)* 46

GREEN PAPAYA SALAD, *(Som Tom)* 47

STRING BEAN SALAD, *(Yaam Thua Poo)* 48

MIXED VEGETABLE SALAD, *(Yaam Yai)* 49

CABBAGE SALAD, *(Salad Galam)* 50

CUCUMBER SALAD, *(Yaam Taeng Kwa)* 51

MIXED FRUIT SALAD, *(Yaam Chomphu)* 52

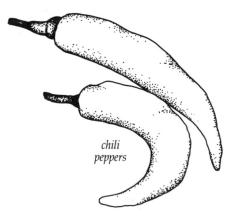

*chili
peppers*

Spicy Prawn Salad
(Yaam Goong)

- 1 head green leaf lettuce, cut into 1-inch squares
- 1 lb medium prawns, shelled, deveined, and boiled (See diagram, page 116.)
- 1/2 inch piece fresh ginger, cut very thinly into julienne strips
- 1 small red onion, thinly sliced
- 2 fresh red chilies, thinly sliced
- 1 stalk lemon grass, very thinly sliced
- 2 cloves garlic, crushed
- 1 tablespoon brown sugar
- 2 tablespoons fish sauce (Nam Pla)
- 1/3 cup fresh lime juice
- 1 teaspoon ground black pepper
- 4 tablespoons green onion, chopped
- 4 tablespoons fresh coriander, chopped
- 15 fresh mint leaves

Put the lettuce in a salad bowl. Arrange the prawns, ginger, onion, and chilies on top. In a bowl, mix the lemon grass, garlic, sugar, fish sauce, lime juice and black pepper. Pour over the salad and garnish with green onion, coriander and mint leaves. **Serves 4-6.**

mint

Dried Shrimp Salad
(Larb)

2 tablespoons vegetable oil

4 cloves garlic, crushed

1 large red onion, chopped

1-1/2 lbs extra lean ground beef

1/4 cup dried shrimp, soaked 3 minutes in warm water, finely chopped

1 teaspoon ground coriander

4 dried red cayenne peppers, chopped

2 tablespoons fresh lime juice

1 teaspoon ground black pepper

4 tablespoons fish sauce (Nam Pla)

4 tablespoons Ground, Toasted Rice (See page 18.)

1 head green iceberg lettuce, or 1 small green cabbage, cut into 1-inch squares

4 tablespoons fresh coriander, chopped

4 tablespoons green onion, chopped

12 mint leaves

Heat the oil in a wok and fry garlic and onion until golden brown. Add the ground beef and dried shrimp and stir-fry for 8 minutes. Add the coriander, cayenne peppers, lime juice, pepper, fish sauce and toasted rice. Stir for 2 more minutes. Place meat on a bed of lettuce or green cabbage. Garnish with fresh coriander, green onion and mint leaves. **Serves 4-6.**

THAI SQUID SALAD
(Yaam Pla Mouk)

1 head green leaf lettuce, cut into 1-inch squares

1 lb. squid, cleaned (See diagram, page 115.), boiled (about 5 minutes), and thinly sliced

1/2 cup fresh mint leaves, chopped

1 small red onion, thinly sliced

1/4 cup green onion, chopped

1 teaspoon salt

2 tablespoons fish sauce (Nam Pla)

1/2 teaspoon dried cayenne pepper flakes

1 teaspoon white sugar

2 tablespoons fresh lemon grass, finely minced

4 tablespoons fresh lime juice

2 fresh hot red chilies, cut into julienne strips

4 tablespoons fresh coriander leaves, chopped

Place the lettuce leaves on a large serving platter and arrange in layers the squid, mint, red onion, and green onion. In a small bowl, mix the salt, fish sauce, cayenne flakes, sugar, lemon grass, lime juice and chilies. Pour the dressing over the salad and garnish with fresh coriander leaves. **Serves 4-6.**

onions

THAI BEEF SALAD
(Yaam Nuea)

1 lb tenderloin beef

2 tablespoons vegetable oil

3 cloves garlic, crushed

2 tablespoons sugar

1 tablespoon fish sauce (Nam Pla)

1 teaspoon salt

2 tablespoons fresh lime juice

1 teaspoon ground black pepper

1 head green leaf lettuce, cut into 1-inch squares

1 red onion, thinly sliced

1 cucumber, peeled, thinly sliced

1 large red tomato, cut into 6 wedges

1/8 cup fresh mint leaves

1/4 cup fresh coriander, chopped

4 tablespoons green onion, chopped

4 fresh red chilies, cut into julienne strips

4 tablespoons Ground Toasted Rice (See page 18.)

Charcoal broil the beef and cut it into small thin slices. In a small frying pan with oil, stir-fry the garlic until golden brown. Add the sugar, fish sauce, salt, lime juice, pepper, and sliced beef. Saute for 2 minutes. Remove the beef and allow to cool. Place the lettuce leaves on a plate and add the beef, onions, cucumbers, tomatoes, mint, coriander, green onion, chilies, and Ground Toasted Rice. Toss and serve. **Serves 4-6.**

GREEN PAPAYA SALAD
(Som Tom)

1 cup green cabbage, cut into 1-inch squares

2 cups grated green papaya (Do not use those beginning to ripen.)

1/2 lb string beans, cut into julienne strips

1/2 cup dried shrimp, thinly sliced

3 cloves garlic, minced

3 dried red chilies, finely chopped

1 tablespoon white sugar

3 tablespoons fish sauce (Nam Pla)

3 tablespoons fresh lime juice

3 small red tomatoes, cut into 4 wedges each

5 tablespoons whole peanuts, roasted, unsalted, crushed in a blender

4 tablespoons fresh coriander leaves, chopped

Place the green cabbage pieces on a large serving platter and arrange in layers the papaya, beans, and shrimp. In a small bowl, mix the garlic, chilies, sugar, fish sauce, and lime juice. Just before serving, pour the dressing over the salad and garnish with tomatoes, peanuts and fresh coriander. **Serves 4-6.**

String Bean Salad
(Yaam Thua Poo)

1 lb string beans, blanched, cut into thin diagonal slices

1/4 lb small cooked shrimp

1/2 lb cooked chicken breast, cut into small cubes

2 green chilies, cut into julienne strips

2 red chilies, cut into julienne strips

1/2 cup coconut milk

2 tablespoons fish sauce (Nam Pla)

4 tablespoons fresh lime juice

2 tablespoons white sugar

1 tablespoon Red Chili Sauce (See page 15.)

Place the string beans on a large serving platter and arrange in layers the shrimp, chicken and green and red chilies. In a small bowl, mix the coconut milk, fish sauce, lime juice, sugar and chili sauce. Just before serving, pour the dressing over the salad. **Serves 4-6.**

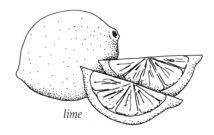

lime

48

MIXED VEGETABLE SALAD
(Yaam Yai)

1 small head lettuce, cut into 1-inch squares

1 cucumber, peeled, very thinly sliced

1 small green papaya, seeded, cut into julienne strips

2 red tomatoes, each cut into 6 wedges

1/4 lb boiled pork loin, thinly sliced

1/2 lb cooked small shrimp

4 tablespoons green onion, chopped

1 boiled egg, quartered

4 tablespoons fresh coriander, chopped

4 tablespoons roasted peanuts, crushed in a blender

2 fresh red chilies, cut into julienne strips

1/4 cup lime juice

1/4 cup fish sauce (Nam Pla)

2 teaspoons sugar

In a large salad bowl, arrange in layers the lettuce, cucumber, papaya, tomatoes, pork, shrimp, green onion, egg and coriander. In a small bowl, mix the peanuts, chilies, lime juice, fish sauce and sugar. Pour over the salad and toss. **Serves 4.**

CABBAGE SALAD
(Salad Galam)

1 small green cabbage, very thinly sliced (about 2 cups)

4 red tomatoes, each cut into 6 wedges

2 carrots, finely grated

1 tablespoon fresh lime peel

2 tablespoons dried, medium shrimp, ground in a mortar

1 tablespoon garlic, crushed

1 tablespoon white sugar

4 tablespoons fresh lime juice

4 tablespoons fish sauce (Nam Pla)

4 tablespoons roasted peanuts, ground in chunks

5 tablespoons fresh coriander, chopped

1 tablespoon dried, hot red chili, crushed

In a large salad bowl, arrange in layers the cabbage, tomatoes, and carrots. In a small bowl, mix the lime peel, dried shrimp, garlic, sugar, lime juice and fish sauce. Pour over the salad and garnish with peanuts, coriander and chili. **Serves 4-6.**

CUCUMBER SALAD
(Yaam Taeng Kwa)

2 cups cucumbers, peeled and sliced

1 red onion, thinly sliced

2 hot red chilies, thinly sliced

3 tablespoons white sugar

3 tablespoons rice vinegar

1/2 cup warm water

On a serving platter, arrange cucumbers, red onion, and chilies in layers. In a bowl, mix the sugar, vinegar, and water and stir until sugar is dissolved. Pour over cucumbers. **Serves 2.**

chili peppers

MIXED FRUIT SALAD
(Yaam Chomphu)

1 green apple, peeled,
   finely sliced

1 green mango, peeled,
   seeded, finely sliced

1 cup pineapple, finely
   sliced

1/2 lb cooked small shrimp

4 tablespoons fresh
   coriander, chopped

1/4 cup lime juice

1/4 cup fish sauce (Nam
   Pla)

2 tablespoons sugar

1 fresh red chili, cut into
   julienne strips

In a large salad bowl, arrange in layers the apple, mango, pineapple, pork, shrimp and coriander. In a small bowl, mix the lime juice, fish sauce, sugar and chili. Pour over the salad and toss. **Serves 4.**

CHAPTER FIVE

VEGETABLES

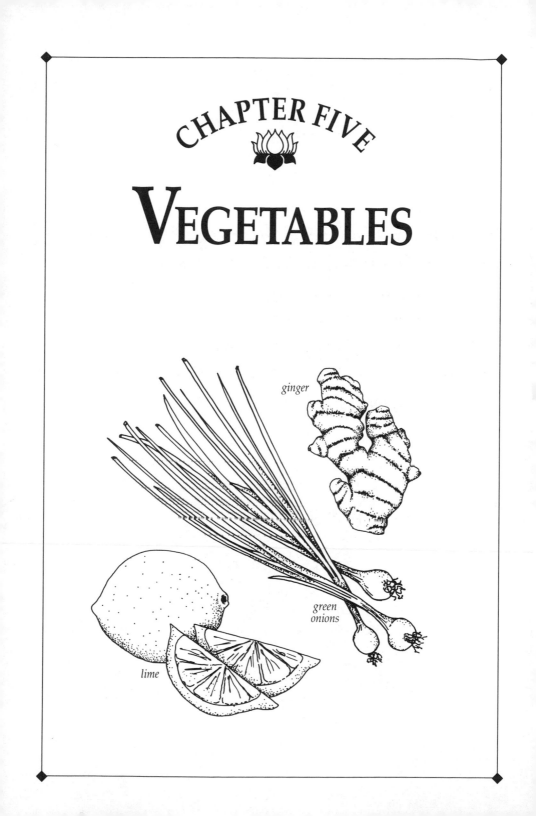

ginger

green onions

lime

CHAPTER FIVE

VEGETABLES

HOT & SOUR STIR-FRIED VEGETABLES, *(Pad Pak Priew Waan)* 55

STIR-FRIED SPINACH, *(Pad Pak Kanar)* 56

STIR-FRIED BEAN SPROUTS & TOFU, *(Thua Ngok Pad Tao Hoo)* ...57

BROCCOLI IN OYSTER SAUCE, *(Pad Pak Naam Mun Hoy)* 58

BEAN SPROUTS WITH TOMATOES, *(Pad Thua-Ngok Saiee Makuatae)* 58

TOFU WITH MIXED VEGETABLES, *(Pad Pak Tao Hoo)* 59

STIR-FRIED MIXED VEGETABLES, *(Pad Pak Ruamit)* 60

SPINACH WITH PEANUT SAUCE, *(Kanar Lad Nam Chim Satay)* 61

STUFFED ZUCCHINI, *(Fang Taeng)* 62

*sweet
basil*

HOT & SOUR STIR-FRIED VEGETABLES
(Pad Pak Priew Waan)

4 tablespoons vegetable oil

1 teaspoon fresh ginger, finely chopped

3 cloves garlic, crushed

1 small red onion, chopped

1 cup carrots, thinly sliced

1 cup green beans, diagonally sliced

1/2 cup green cabbage, cut into one-inch squares

1 cup zucchini, thinly sliced

1 teaspoon salt

3 teaspoons white sugar

1 tablespoon soy sauce

2 tablespoons fish sauce (Nam Pla)

2 tablespoons fresh lime juice

1 fresh hot red cayenne, thinly sliced

2 tablespoons green onion, chopped

4 tablespoons fresh coriander, chopped

In a wok with oil, fry the ginger, garlic, and onion until soft. Add the carrots and green beans. Stir-fry for 2 minutes. Then add the cabbage, zucchini, salt, sugar, soy sauce, fish sauce, lime juice, and cayenne. Stir for another 2 minutes until all the vegetables are tender, but not overcooked. Garnish with green onion and coriander. **Serves 4-6.**

STIR-FRIED SPINACH
(Pad Pak Kanar)

6 tablespoons vegetable oil

4 cloves garlic, crushed

2 tablespoons soy bean paste

1 teaspoon ground black pepper

2 red tomatoes, each cut into 6 wedges

2 fresh hot red chilies, sliced

2 lbs fresh spinach, chopped

Heat the oil in a wok and stir-fry the garlic, soy bean paste, pepper, tomatoes, and chilies for 1 minute. Add the spinach and cook for 3 minutes, stirring frequently. Serve hot. Do not overcook. **Serves 4.**

STIR-FRIED BEAN SPROUTS & TOFU
(Thua Ngok Pad Tao Hoo)

4 tablespoons vegetable oil

3 cloves garlic, crushed

2 red tomatoes, cut into 4 wedges

1 pkg. fried tofu (4 oz.), cut into cubes, (See glossary, page 122.)

1 lb bean sprouts

2 fresh hot red chilies, sliced

1/4 cup green onion, chopped

1 teaspoon salt

1 teaspoon black pepper

2 tablespoons oyster sauce

4 tablespoons fresh coriander leaves, chopped

Heat the oil in a wok and stir-fry the garlic until brown. Add the tomatoes, bean curd, bean sprouts, chilies, green onion, salt, black pepper, and oyster sauce. Stir-fry for 2 minutes. Serve hot. Garnish with fresh coriander leaves. **Serves 4.**

chili peppers

BROCCOLI IN OYSTER SAUCE
(Pad Pak Naam Mun Hoy)

4 tablespoons vegetable oil

3 cloves garlic, crushed

1 lb fresh broccoli, cut into small florets (Discard the tough stems.)

6 tablespoons oyster sauce

Heat the oil in a wok and stir-fry the garlic until brown. Add the broccoli and stir-fry for 3 minutes over low heat. Then, add the oyster sauce and stir for 1 more minute. Transfer to a serving dish and serve hot. **Serves 4.**

BEAN SPROUTS WITH TOMATOES
(Pad Thua-Ngok Saiee Makuatae)

4 tablespoons vegetable oil

4 gloves garlic

2 tablespoons soy bean paste

1 yellow onion, quartered

4 cups bean sprouts

1 red chili pepper, thinly sliced

3 red tomatoes, quartered

4 tablespoons green onion, chopped

4 tablespoons fresh coriander leaves

Heat the oil in a wok and stir-fry the garlic and soy bean paste for 1 minute. Add the onion, bean sprouts, chili and tomatoes. Cook for 2 minutes, stirring frequently. Garnish with green onion and fresh coriander leaves. Serve hot. **Serves 4.**

TOFU WITH MIXED VEGETABLES
(Pad Pak Tao Hoo)

6 tablespoons vegetable oil

3 cloves garlic, crushed

1 yellow onion, quartered

1 cup Japanese eggplant, cut into 1-inch cubes

1 pkg. tofu (14.2 oz.), cut into 1-inch cubes

1 cup zucchini, thinly sliced

1 tomato, quartered

2 red chili peppers, thinly sliced

12 sweet basil leaves

In a wok with oil over medium heat, stir fry the garlic until golden brown. Add the onion, eggplant and tofu and cook for 5 minutes. Add the zucchini, tomato and red chili peppers. Stir well for 1 minute. Garnish with sweet basil leaves. **Serves 4-6.**

STIR-FRIED MIXED VEGETABLES
(Pad Pak Ruamit)

4 tablespoons vegetable oil

4 cloves garlic, crushed

1 cup fresh string beans,
  cut into 2-inch lengths

1 cup Japanese eggplant,
  cut into 1-inch cubes

1 cup chopped green
  cabbage

1 can straw mushrooms,
  drained (15 oz.)

1 can baby corn (15 oz.)

1/2 cup bamboo shoots, cut
  into julienne strips

2 red chili peppers, thinly
  sliced

1 stalk fresh lemon grass,
  cut into 2-inch lengths

6 kaffir lime leaves

1 can coconut milk
  (14 fl. oz.)

2 teaspoons salt

20 sweet basil leaves

In a wok, heat the oil over high heat and stir-fry the garlic, string beans and eggplant for 3 minutes. Add the cabbage, straw mushrooms, baby corn, bamboo shoots, red chili peppers, lemon grass, kaffir lime leaves, coconut milk, and salt. Cook for 2 minutes. Add the basil and stir well. Serve hot.
Serves 4-6.

SPINACH WITH PEANUT SAUCE
(Kanar Lad Nam Chim Satay)

2 lbs spinach, cleaned, and washed

3 tablespoons rice flour

2 tablespoons cornstarch

2 cups vegetable oil for deep-frying

1 pkg. tofu (14.2 oz.), cut into 1-inch cubes

1 cup Satay Peanut Sauce (See page 15.)

1 tablespoon crushed red chili pepper

2 tablespoons ground roasted peanuts

4 tablespoons fresh coriander leaves

Blanch the spinach and drain well. Set aside. Combine rice flour and cornstarch. Preheat oil for deep-frying over medium heat. Coat tofu with rice flour mixture. Deep-fry for 5 minutes or until golden brown. Drain on a paper towel. On a serving platter, place the spinach and fried tofu and pour Satay Peanut Sauce on top. Then garnish with chili, peanuts, and fresh coriander leaves. **Serves 4-6.**

onions

STUFFED ZUCCHINI
(Fang Taeng)

1 green zucchini, about 10 inches long

1/2 lb ground pork

1 can crab meat (6-1/2 oz.), drained

3 cloves garlic, crushed

1 teaspoon ground white pepper

1 teaspoon sugar

1 fresh hot red chili, cut into julienne strips

4 tablespoons fish sauce (Nam Pla)

4 tablespoons fresh coriander leaves

Cut off the ends of the zucchini and remove pith and seeds with a small teaspoon. Thoroughly mix the pork, crab meat, garlic, pepper, sugar, chili and fish sauce. Stuff the mixture into the zucchini cylinder. Replace the ends of the zucchini and place in a steamer for 20 minutes or until cooked. Cool and slice in rounds about 1-inch in length. Garnish with coriander leaves. **Serves 2-4.**

CHAPTER SIX

SEAFOOD

*kaffir
lime leaves*

garlic

*coriander
or cilantro*

CHAPTER SIX

✤

SEAFOOD

SPICY STEAMED MUSSELS, *(Haw Mog Hoy)* 65

STIR-FRIED CLAMS WITH BASIL, *(Hoy Lai Pad Horapa)* 66

FRIED SQUID WITH HOT SAUCE, *(Pla Mueg Pad Prig)* 67

STUFFED CRAB SHELLS, *(Poo Ja)* 68

SWEET AND SOUR SHRIMP, *(Pad Priew Waan Goong)* 69

GREEN CURRY WITH PRAWNS, *(Gaeng Khiaw-waan Goong)* 70

SAUTED SHRIMP WITH LEMON GRASS, *(Pad Pak Goong)* 71

SHRIMP WITH GARLIC, *(Gaeng Kua Goong)* 72

CRISPY FRIED CATFISH, *(Yaam Pla Dook)* 73

FISH WITH RED SAUCE, *(Pla Nhung)* 74

CRISPY FRIED SNAPPER, *(Pla Grapong Thod Foo)* 75

FRIED FISH WITH TAMARIND, *(Pla Tod Lad Prik Mak Kam)* 76

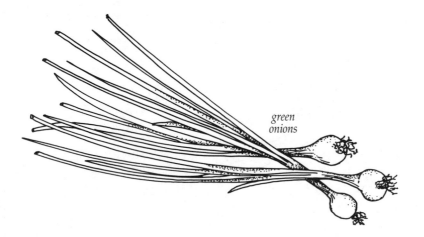

green onions

SPICY STEAMED MUSSELS
(Haw Mog Hoy)

2 lbs fresh mussels, washed, drained

4 tablespoons vegetable oil

1 yellow onion, finely chopped

4 cloves garlic, crushed

2 fresh red chilies, sliced

4 tablespoons fresh coriander, chopped

1 one-inch piece dried galangal (or 1 teaspoon ground)

1 stalk fresh lemon grass, cut into 2-inch lengths

2 tablespoons fresh lime juice

1 teaspoon shrimp paste (Kapi)

1/2 cup coconut milk

1 egg, beaten

1 teaspoon salt

2 teaspoons ground white pepper

2 tablespoons rice flour

20 fresh holy or sweet basil leaves

Place the mussels in a steamer and bring the water to a boil. Steam for 2 minutes or until the mussels open. (Discard mussels that do not open.) Remove the mussels from the shells, retaining the larger shells. In a wok, heat the oil and saute the onion and garlic until golden brown. Next, add the chilies, coriander, galangal, lemon grass, lime juice, and shrimp paste and cook for 2 minutes. Pour the sauce in a bowl and add the coconut milk, egg, salt, pepper and rice flour. Arrange the holy basil leaves in the bottom of the retained shells. Place 2 to 3 mussels in each shell and spoon a little sauce on top of each. Place in a steamer and cook for 2 more minutes or until hot. Serve hot. **Serves 4-6.**

STIR-FRIED CLAMS WITH BASIL
(Hoy Lai Pad Horapa)

4 tablespoons vegetable oil

8 cloves garlic, crushed

1 yellow onion, finely
chopped

6 fresh green chilies, thinly
sliced

1/2 cup fresh sweet basil
leaves

2 lbs fresh clams, washed,
drained

1/2 cup fish sauce
(Nam Pla)

4 fresh hot red chilies,
shredded

2 tablespoons fresh lime
juice

In a wok with oil, saute the garlic, onion, green chilies, and basil leaves until brown. Add the clams and fish sauce and stir-fry for 4 minutes over high heat, frequently stirring. Pour into a large serving platter and garnish with red chilies and lime juice. **Serves 4-6.**

FRIED SQUID WITH HOT SAUCE
(Pla Mueg Pad Prig)

1 1/2 lbs fresh squid, cleaned (See diagram, page 115.)

4 tablespoons vegetable oil

1 large yellow onion, finely chopped

4 cloves garlic, crushed

2 fresh red chilies, thinly sliced

1 teaspoon fresh ginger, thinly sliced

1 tablespoon fish sauce (Nam Pla)

1 tablespoon oyster sauce

2 tablespoons rice wine

1 teaspoon salt

1 teaspoon brown sugar

1 teaspoon ground white pepper

4 tablespoons fresh coriander, chopped

Partially cook the squid by simmering it for 3 minutes in a small pot. Drain and set aside. Heat the oil in a wok and saute the onion, garlic, chilies, and ginger until golden brown. Add the squid, fish sauce, oyster sauce, wine, salt, sugar and pepper and continue cooking until the squid is cooked, about one minute. Garnish with coriander leaves. Serve hot. **Serves 4-6.**

STUFFED CRAB SHELLS
(Poo Ja)

4 medium-sized, cooked
  crabs

1/2 lb ground pork

1 small yellow onion,
  finely chopped

3 cloves garlic, crushed

2 teaspoons fresh ginger,
  finely chopped

4 tablespoons fresh
  coriander, finely chopped

1/2 cup coconut milk

3 tablespoons cornstarch

1 egg, beaten

1 teaspoon salt

1 teaspoon ground black
  pepper

2 cups vegetable oil for
  deep-frying

Carefully extract all the meat from body and claws of crabs and shred finely. Save shells. In a bowl, place crab meat, ground pork, onion, garlic, ginger, coriander, coconut milk, cornstarch, egg, salt, and black pepper. Mix thoroughly. Stuff crab shells with mixture and place in steamer for 30 minutes. Remove, set aside and allow to cool. After shells have cooled, heat oil in a wok and deep-fry stuffed shells for 3 minutes or until top is golden brown. **Serves 4.**

ginger

SWEET AND SOUR SHRIMP
(Pad Priew Waan Goong)

1 lb medium-sized prawns, shelled, deveined (See diagram, page 116.)

2 teaspoons salt

1 teaspoon ground white pepper

1 teaspoon white sugar

3 tablespoons fresh lime juice

2 tablespoons rice wine

4 tablespoons vegetable oil

3 cloves garlic, crushed

1 yellow onion, finely chopped

1 green bell pepper, cut into 1-inch squares

1 red sweet bell pepper, cut into 1-inch squares

1 tablespoon brown sugar

2 tablespoons tomato paste

1/2 cup water

1/4 cup pineapple, cut into 1/2 inch squares

2 tablespoons cornstarch, dissolved in 1 tablespoon water

6 tablespoons fresh coriander, chopped

In a small bowl, season the shrimp with salt, pepper, sugar, lime juice, and wine. Let marinate for 5 minutes. Heat the oil in a large wok and saute the garlic and onion until golden brown. Add the shrimp and stir for 2 minutes. Add the green and red pepper, brown sugar, tomato paste, and water. Stir well and bring to a boil. Add the pineapple pieces. Cook over a moderate heat for 2 minutes. Slowly add the cornstarch dissolved in water to the mixture and stir well. Garnish with fresh coriander leaves. Serve hot. **Serves 4.**

GREEN CURRY WITH PRAWNS
(Gaeng Khiaw-waan Goong)

4 tablespoons vegetable oil

1 yellow onion, chopped

4 tablespoons Green Curry Paste (See page 20.)

8 kaffir lime leaves

2 lbs fresh medium-sized prawns, shelled, deveined (See diagram, page 116.)

2 tablespoons brown sugar

1 can coconut milk (14 fl. oz.)

10 fresh basil leaves

2 tablespoons fresh coriander, chopped

Heat the oil in a wok and stir-fry the onion until golden brown. Add the curry paste, kaffir lime leaves, prawns and sugar. Simmer for 5 minutes and add the coconut milk. Bring back to a boil for 2 more minutes. Garnish with basil and coriander leaves. **Serves 4-6.**

SAUTED SHRIMP WITH LEMON GRASS
(Pad Pak Goong)

4 tablespoons vegetable oil

5 cloves garlic, crushed

1 large red onion, thinly sliced

1 stalk lemon grass, cut into 2-inch lengths

1 tablespoon salt

2 lbs large shrimp, shelled and deveined (See diagram, page 116.)

4 tablespoons green onion, chopped

4 tablespoons fresh coriander, chopped

2 fresh hot red chilies, cut into julienne strips

Heat the oil at medium high in a wok and stir-fry the garlic, onion and lemon grass for a few seconds until the aroma is released. Add salt and increase the heat to high. Add the shrimp and stir-fry for 3 minutes. Pour onto a serving platter and sprinkle with the green onion, coriander and chilies. **Serves 4-6.**

lemon grass

SHRIMP WITH GARLIC
(Gaeng Kua Goong)

4 tablespoons vegetable oil

4 cloves garlic, crushed

2 lbs medium shrimp, shelled and deveined (See diagram, page 116.)

1 can coconut milk (14 fl. oz.)

1 can straw mushrooms, drained (15 oz.)

1 teaspoon ground white pepper

2 tablespoons fish sauce (Nam Pla)

4 tablespoons fresh coriander

In a medium pot with oil over medium heat, stir-fry garlic until golden brown. Add shrimp and stir for 3 minutes. Add the coconut milk, straw mushrooms, white pepper and fish sauce. Cook for about 10 more minutes or until shrimp is cooked. Garnish with fresh coriander leaves. **Serves 4-6.**

garlic

CRISPY FRIED CATFISH
(Yaam Pla Dook)

2 lbs catfish fillets

2 cups vegetable oil for deep-frying

2 unripe (green) mangos, peeled and seeded, cut into julienne strips

10 cloves garlic, thinly sliced and fried in 4 tablespoons vegetable oil until crisp

1 tablespoon finely shredded fresh ginger

2 tablespoons palm sugar or brown sugar

2 tablespoons fish sauce (Nam Pla)

2 tablespoons fresh lime juice

2 red chili peppers, thinly sliced

4 tablespoons fresh coriander leaves

In a steamer, steam fish fillets for 8 minutes until opaque and just tender. Let cool. Cut fish into 2-inch squares. Heat oil in a wok over medium heat and fry the fish until crisp and well browned. Drain on paper towels. Set aside. In a small bowl, mix mangoes, garlic and ginger. Mound the mixture in the center of a serving platter. Surround it with fried fish. Combine the sugar, fish sauce and lime juice in a cup and stir until sugar dissolves. Sprinkle most of the sauce over mango mixture and the remainder over the fish. Garnish with red chili peppers and fresh coriander leaves. **Serves 6-8.**

FISH WITH RED SAUCE
(Pla Nhung)

6 tablespoons vegetable oil

2 yellow onions, finely chopped

3 cloves garlic, crushed

6 red tomatoes, peeled and chopped

2 tablespoons fresh lime juice

4 tablespoons fish sauce (Nam Pla)

1 teaspoon ground white pepper

2 red chili peppers, thinly sliced

2 lbs sea bass, cut into 2-inch squares

4 tablespoons fresh coriander leaves

In a large pot with oil over medium-high heat, fry the onions and garlic until golden brown. Add the tomatoes, lime juice, fish sauce, white pepper, and chilies. Cover and simmer for 15 minutes or until the sauce is thick. Add the fish, cover and cook for 10 minutes or until fish is cooked. Garnish with fresh coriander leaves. **Serves 6-8.**

CRISPY FRIED SNAPPER
(Pla Grapong Thod Foo)

1 lb red snapper

2 cloves garlic, crushed

2 tablespoons fresh lime juice

1 teaspoon white sugar

1 teaspoon ground white pepper

2 tablespoons cornstarch

2 cups vegetable oil for frying

1 fresh red chili, shredded

In a bowl, marinate the fish for 5 minutes with garlic, lime juice, sugar, and pepper. Coat the fish with cornstarch. Heat the oil in a wok and deep-fry the fish until golden brown on both sides. Remove from the oil and garnish with shredded chili. **Serves 4-6.**

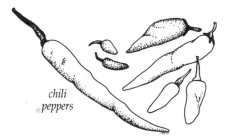

chili peppers

FRIED FISH WITH TAMARIND
(Pla Tod Lad Prik Mak Kam)

2 lbs whole snapper, cleaned and scaled

1 teaspoon salt

2 tablespoons rice flour

3 cups vegetable oil (for deep-frying)

2 tablespoons vegetable oil (for sauteing garlic)

4 cloves garlic, crushed

3 tablespoons soy sauce

1 tablespoon palm sugar or brown sugar

3 tablespoons fish sauce (Nam Pla)

4 tablespoons tamarind liquid

1 tablespoon finely shredded fresh ginger

4 green onions, cut into 1-inch lengths

4 tablespoons fresh coriander leaves

4 fresh red chilies, thinly sliced

Wash the fish and dry well. Diagonally score fish on both sides every 1-inch, cutting halfway to the bone. Coat fish with salt and rice flour. Heat the oil in a large wok over medium heat and deep-fry on each side for 10 minutes or until fish is cooked and crispy, but not overcooked. Drain on a paper towel. In a small pot with oil over low heat, fry the garlic until golden brown. Add the soy sauce, sugar, fish sauce, tamarind liquid and bring to a boil. Add the ginger, and green onions and cook for 1 minute. Pour the sauce over the fish and garnish with fresh coriander leaves and red chilies. Serve hot. **Serves 6-8.**

CHAPTER SEVEN

MEAT & POULTRY

ginger

chili peppers

sweet basil

CHAPTER SEVEN
MEAT & POULTRY

GREEN CURRY WITH BEEF, *(Gang Khiaw-waan Nuea)* 79

ORANGE BEEF, *(Sum Nuea)* 80

SPICY FRIED GINGER BEEF, *(Pad Pet Nuea King)* 81

STIR-FRIED BEEF WITH CHILIES, *(Pad Prig Nuea)* 82

STIR-FRIED BEEF WITH BASIL, *(Pad Nuea Bye Ga Pon)* 83

PANAENG BEEF CURRY, *(Panaeng Nuea)* 84

BEEF CURRY WITH EGGPLANT, *(Gaeng Gari Nuea)* 85

PORK BALLS & VEGETABLES, *(Pad Loog Chin)* 86

RED CURRY WITH PORK, *(Gang Pet Mu)* 87

CHICKEN CURRY, *(Gaeng Pet Gai)* 88

CHICKEN WITH BLACK MUSHROOMS, *(Tom Kem Gai)* 89

STUFFED CHICKEN BREASTS, *(Og Gai Sod Sai)* 90

SPICY GROUND CHICKEN, *(Laab Gai)* 91

CHICKEN MASAMAN CURRY, *(Gaeng Daeng Gai)* 92

THAI BARBECUE CHICKEN, *(Gai Yaang)* 93

FRIED CHICKEN IN PANDANUS LEAVES, *(Gai Haw Bai Toey)* 94

CHICKEN WITH EGGPLANT, *(Pad Makua Gai)* 95

CHICKEN BREAST WITH CASHEW, *(Pad Gai Met Mamuang Himapan)* 95

AROMATIC FRIED CHICKEN, *(Gai Tord)* 96

GREEN CURRY WITH BEEF
(Gang Khiaw-waan Nuea)

4 tablespoons vegetable oil

1/2 cup Green Curry Paste
(See page 20.)

1 lb top sirloin beef, thinly
sliced

1 can coconut milk
(14 fl. oz.)

4 kaffir lime leaves

1 tablespoon brown sugar

1 tablespoon fish sauce
(Nam Pla)

2 tablespoons light soy
sauce

4 tablespoons fresh sweet
basil leaves

4 tablespoons fresh
coriander leaves,
chopped

Heat the oil in a pot over medium heat. Add the curry paste and stir for 2 minutes. Add the beef and stir-fry for 3 minutes. Add the coconut milk and lime leaves and bring to a boil. Reduce the heat and add the sugar, fish sauce, and soy sauce. Cook for 2 more minutes. Garnish with basil and coriander. **Serves 4-6.**

ORANGE BEEF
(Sum Nuea)

1 lb tenderloin beef, thinly sliced

3 cloves garlic, crushed

1 teaspoon salt

1 teaspoon ground white pepper

3 tablespoons tapioca flour

1 cup vegetable oil (for deep-frying)

1 tablespoon vegetable oil (for stir-frying)

2 fresh oranges, peels only (*See below.)

1/2 cup dark soy sauce

1/4 cup white sugar

4 tablespoons rice vinegar

2 tablespoons dried, hot red chilies, crushed

* Gently grate the outer peel off the oranges. Try not to grate too deeply.

In a small bowl, marinate the beef for 5 minutes with garlic, salt, and pepper. Coat the sliced beef on both sides with tapioca flour. Heat the oil in a wok and deep-fry the sliced beef until golden brown. Remove the crispy beef from the wok, drain on paper towels and set aside. In a frying pan with oil, saute the orange peel over medium heat for 1 minute. Add the crispy beef and stir-fry for 1 more minute. Set aside. In a small sauce pan, simmer uncovered the soy sauce, sugar, and rice vinegar over a low heat for 10 minutes. Place the crispy beef with orange peel on a serving platter and pour the sauce over the mixture. Garnish with the dried chilies. **Serves 4.**

SPICY FRIED GINGER BEEF
(Pad Pet Nuea King)

4 tablespoons vegetable oil

4 cloves garlic, crushed

1 fresh green chili, thinly sliced

1 fresh hot red chili, thinly sliced

1 one-inch piece fresh ginger, cut into julienne strips

1 lb top sirloin beef, thinly sliced

1 tablespoon fresh lime juice

1 tablespoon fish sauce (Nam Pla)

1 teaspoon sugar

2 tablespoons fresh coriander leaves

2 tablespoons green onion, chopped

Heat the oil in a wok over medium heat. Stir-fry the garlic, green chili, red chili, and ginger until golden brown. Add the beef, and stir-fry for 2 minutes. Add the lime juice, fish sauce, and sugar and stir for 1 more minute. Garnish with coriander and green onion. **Serves 4.**

ginger

STIR-FRIED BEEF WITH CHILIES
(Pad Prig Nuea)

4 tablespoons vegetable oil

1 yellow onion, thinly sliced

3 cloves garlic, crushed

4 fresh red chilies, cut into julienne strips

1 lb tenderloin beef, thinly sliced

4 dried black mushrooms, soaked in 1/8 cup of warm water for 10 minutes (Save the water.), cut into julienne strips (Note: Discard hard ends from stems.)

2 tablespoons light soy sauce

2 tablespoons oyster sauce

1 tablespoon rice wine

6 tablespoons fresh coriander, chopped

Heat the oil in a wok and stir-fry the onion and garlic until golden brown. Add the chilies and beef. Stir for 4 minutes. Add the mushrooms along with soaking water, soy sauce, oyster sauce, and wine. Reduce the heat and stir for 2 minutes. Garnish with fresh coriander. **Serves 4.**

STIR-FRIED BEEF WITH BASIL
(Pad Nuea Bye Ga Pon)

4 tablespoons vegetable oil

3 cloves garlic, crushed

1 lb tenderloin beef, thinly sliced

1 small red onion, sliced

1/2 cup fresh mushrooms, sliced

2 fresh hot red cayenne peppers, sliced

3 tablespoons fish sauce (Nam Pla)

1 teaspoon sugar

15 holy or sweet basil leaves

In a large wok, heat the oil over high heat and stir-fry the garlic and beef for 2 minutes. Add the onions, mushrooms, cayenne, fish sauce, sugar and holy basil. Stir well for 2 minutes. Serve hot over rice. **Serves 4.**

*sweet
basil*

PANAENG BEEF CURRY
(Panaeng Nuea)

2 cans coconut milk
  (14 fl. oz. each)

1 lb top sirloin, cut into
  1-inch cubes

2 cloves garlic, crushed

1 teaspoon ground
  coriander

1 teaspoon salt

1 teaspoon white pepper

1 stalk lemon grass, cut
  into 2-inch lengths, or
  1 teaspoon ground lemon
  grass

2 tablespoons fish sauce
  (Nam Pla)

2 tablespoons chunky
  peanut butter

1 tablespoon brown sugar

1 one-inch piece dried
  galangal (Kha)

12 sweet basil leaves for
  garnishing

In a large pot, bring coconut milk to a boil over high heat, stirring occasionally. Reduce to low and simmer uncovered for 15 minutes, stirring occasionally. Once coconut milk has thickened, add remaining ingredients except for the basil leaves, and stir. Cover pot and simmer over medium heat for 1 hour, or until beef is tender. Garnish with basil leaves. **Serves 4-6.**

Beef Curry with Eggplant
(Gaeng Gari Nuea)

4 tablespoons vegetable oil

6 dried red chilies, soaked, drained, finely chopped

1 yellow onion, chopped

3 cloves garlic, crushed

1 one-inch piece dried galangal (Kha)

1 stalk fresh lemon grass, cut into 2-inch lengths

4 kaffir lime leaves

1 teaspoon ground cumin

1 tablespoon ground coriander

1/2 teaspoon dried, sweet basil

1 lb top sirloin beef, thinly sliced

1 small eggplant, cut into 1-inch cubes

1 can coconut milk (14 fl. oz.)

3 tablespoons fish sauce (Nam Pla)

12 fresh sweet basil leaves

2 fresh red chilies, thinly sliced

Heat the oil in a deep pot over medium heat and stir-fry the chilies, onion, garlic, galangal, lemon grass, lime leaves, cumin, coriander, and dry basil for 2 minutes. Then, add the beef, eggplant, coconut milk, and fish sauce. Simmer for 10 minutes or until the beef is tender. Garnish with fresh basil leaves and sliced chilies. **Serves 4-6.**

chili peppers

PORK BALLS & VEGETABLES
(Pad Loog Chin)

1 lb ground pork

2 dried black mushrooms, soaked in 1/8 cup warm water for 10 minutes, (Discard water.), cut into julienne strips (Note: Discard hard ends from stems.)

1 yellow onion, chopped

3 cloves garlic, crushed

2 tablespoons fresh coriander, finely chopped

1 tablespoon fresh lime juice

1 teaspoon white sugar

1 teaspoon salt

1 egg, beaten

2 tablespoons white flour

1 cup vegetable oil (for frying pork balls)

2 tablespoons vegetable oil (for stir-frying vegetables)

1 cup Chinese pea pods

1/2 cup bamboo shoots, cut into julienne strips

1/4 cup water chestnuts, thinly sliced

In a small bowl, thoroughly mix the pork, mushrooms, onion, 2 cloves garlic, coriander, lime juice, sugar, salt, egg, and flour. Shape into small balls, one-inch in diameter. Heat the oil in a wok over medium-high heat and deep-fry the meat balls until both sides are golden brown. Remove from the oil and set aside. Heat oil in a frying pan and saute 1 clove garlic, Chinese pea pods, bamboo shoots, and water chestnuts. Stir for 4 minutes and add fried meat balls. Mix well for 1 minute and serve hot. **Serves 4-6.**

RED CURRY WITH PORK
(Gang Pet Mu)

3 tablespoons vegetable oil

1 tablespoon Red Curry
  Paste (See page 21.)

1 lb tenderloin pork, thinly
  sliced

1 cup bamboo shoots, cut
  into julienne strips

4 kaffir lime leaves

1 can coconut milk
  (14 fl. oz.)

4 tablespoons fish sauce
  (Nam Pla)

12 sweet basil leaves

In a medium-sized pot, heat the oil and red curry paste over medium heat for 2 minutes. Add the pork, bamboo shoots, kaffir lime leaves, coconut milk, and fish sauce. Stir well and cook covered for 15 minutes or until pork is tender. Garnish with sweet basil leaves. Serve hot. **Serves 4-6.**

*kaffir
lime leaves*

CHICKEN CURRY
(Gaeng Pet Gai)

4 tablespoons vegetable oil

10 dried red chilies, soaked, drained, chopped

1 yellow onion, chopped

4 cloves garlic, crushed

1 one-inch piece dried, or 1 teaspoon ground, galangal (Kha)

1 stalk fresh lemon grass, cut into 2-inch lengths

4 tablespoons fresh coriander, chopped

1 teaspoon ground nutmeg

6 kaffir lime leaves

1 tablespoon ground coriander

1 teaspoon ground cumin

1 teaspoon salt

2 whole chicken breasts, boned, skinned, cut into 1-inch cubes

1 can bamboo shoots (6 oz.), cut into fine shreds

1 can coconut milk (14 fl. oz.)

20 fresh basil leaves

Heat the oil in a medium-sized pot and stir-fry the chilies, onion, and garlic until brown. Add galangal, lemon grass, fresh coriander, nutmeg, kaffir lime leaves, ground coriander, cumin and salt and cook over medium-high heat for 2 minutes. Add the chicken and stir for 1 minute. Add the bamboo shoots and coconut milk. Simmer for about 20 minutes over low heat or until the chicken is tender. Garnish with fresh basil. **Serves 4-6.**

CHICKEN WITH BLACK MUSHROOMS
(Tom Kem Gai)

10 drumsticks

3 tablespoons rice flour

4 tablespoons vegetable oil

1 yellow onion, finely chopped

3 cloves garlic, crushed

1/2 inch piece fresh ginger, thinly sliced

1 teaspoon ground coriander

1/2 teaspoon salt

1 teaspoon ground black pepper

1/4 cup brown sugar

1/2 cup water

4 tablespoons soy sauce

6 dried black Chinese mushrooms, soaked in 1/4 cup of warm water for 10 minutes, (Save the water.), cut into julienne strips (Note: Discard hard ends from stems.)

6 hard-boiled eggs, shelled

4 tablespoons fresh coriander leaves

In a small bowl, coat the drumsticks with flour. Heat the oil in a medium pot and stir-fry the onion, garlic, ginger, coriander, salt, and pepper for 2 minutes. Add the sugar, water, soy sauce, chicken coated with flour, and black mushrooms and soaking water. Simmer for 30 minutes. Add the hard-boiled eggs and cook slowly for 10 minutes. Garnish with fresh coriander leaves. **Serves 4-6.**

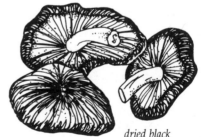

dried black mushrooms

STUFFED CHICKEN BREASTS
(Og Gai Sod Sai)

- 2 whole boneless chicken breasts, skinned
- 3 tablespoons light soy sauce
- 1/4 lb ground pork
- 2 water chestnuts, finely chopped
- 4 fresh mushrooms, finely chopped
- 3 cloves garlic, crushed
- 2 fresh red chilies, finely chopped
- 2 tablespoons fresh coriander, chopped
- 1 egg, beaten
- 3 teaspoons rice flour
- 1/2 teaspoon salt
- 1 teaspoon ground white pepper
- 2 pieces kitchen string (each 6 inches long)
- 2 cups vegetable oil for frying

Slightly flatten the chicken breasts and rub the soy sauce on both sides and set aside for 15 minutes. In a bowl, mix thoroughly the ground pork, water chestnuts, mushrooms, garlic, chilies, coriander, egg, rice flour, salt, and white pepper. Spread the mixture evenly over the chicken breasts. Roll up the breasts and secure with the string. Heat the oil in a wok over medium heat and deep-fry the chicken until tender and golden brown. Before serving the chicken, remove the string. **Serves 4-6.**

SPICY GROUND CHICKEN
(Laab Gai)

4 tablespoons vegetable oil

2 lbs chicken breast, finely chopped (or ground in a food processor)

1 stalk fresh lemon grass, finely chopped

4 tablespoons green onion, chopped

1 red onion, finely sliced

1 teaspoon ground galangal (Kha)

4 tablespoons fish sauce (Nam Pla)

1/4 cup fresh lime juice

2 dried hot red chilies, roasted, crushed

2 tablespoons Ground Toasted Rice (See page 18.)

8 leaves of green leaf lettuce

12 mint leaves

1/4 cup fresh coriander leaves, chopped

Heat the oil over medium heat in a wok and add the chicken. Stir-fry until cooked. Drain the chicken and place it in a mixing bowl and add the lemon grass, green onion, red onion, galangal, fish sauce, lime juice, red chilies, and ground rice. Mix well and set aside. On a bed of lettuce leaves, arrange the chicken mixture and garnish with mint and coriander leaves. **Serves 4-6.**

mint

CHICKEN MASAMAN CURRY
(Gaeng Daeng Gai)

4 tablespoons vegetable oil

1 red onion, finely chopped

3 cloves garlic, crushed

4 lbs drumsticks

1 teaspoon salt

1/2 teaspoon ground cloves

1 teaspoon ground cumin

1 tablespoon ground
coriander

1/2 teaspoon ground
cardamon

1 stalk fresh lemon grass,
cut into 2-inch lengths

1 teaspoon ground
cinnamon

4 bay leaves

1 tablespoon sugar

2 tablespoons fish sauce
(Nam Pla)

1 tablespoon lemon juice

4 dried hot red chilies

1 can coconut milk
(14 fl. oz.)

4 raw potatoes, peeled, cut
into bite-sized pieces

1/2 cup roasted peanuts

Heat the oil in a large pot over medium-high heat and saute the onion and garlic until golden brown. Add the chicken and fry for 5 minutes. Then, add the salt, cloves, cumin, coriander, cardamon, lemon grass, cinnamon, bay leaves, sugar, fish sauce, lemon juice, chilies, coconut milk, and potatoes. Stir and cover, reduce heat to low, and simmer for 30 minutes or until the chicken and potatoes are tender. Garnish with peanuts. **Serves 6-8.**

THAI BARBECUE CHICKEN
(Gai Yaang)

8 cloves garlic, crushed

1 tablespoon ground white pepper

1/2 cup fresh coriander, finely chopped

1 teaspoon salt

1 teaspoon ground coriander

1 tablespoon red chili flakes

2 tablespoons fresh lime juice

4 lbs drumsticks

In a bowl, thoroughly mix the garlic, white pepper, fresh coriander, salt, ground coriander, chili flakes, lime juice, and drumsticks. Marinate for 30 minutes or overnight in a refrigerator. Barbecue over a moderate charcoal fire for 30 minutes or until well-cooked on both sides. Serve with Red Chili Sauce (See page 15.). **Serves 6-8.**

coriander
or cilantro

FRIED CHICKEN IN PANDANUS LEAVES
(Gai Haw Bai Toey)

6 cloves garlic, crushed

1 small red onion, finely chopped

4 tablespoons fresh coriander, finely chopped

2 tablespoons fresh lemon grass, finely chopped

1 teaspoon ground white pepper

1 tablespoon Red Chili Sauce (See page 15.)

2 tablespoons light soy sauce

1 tablespoon dark brown sugar

1/4 cup coconut milk

1/2 teaspoon salt

12 boneless chicken thighs, skinned, cut into 1-inch cubes

1 bunch fresh pandanus leaves

2 cups vegetable oil for frying

In a small bowl, mix thoroughly the garlic, onion, fresh coriander, lemon grass, pepper, red chili sauce, soy sauce, sugar, coconut milk, salt, and chicken cubes. Marinate for 15 minutes or overnight in a refrigerator. In a pandanus leaf, preferrably 1-inch wide, securely wrap one teaspoonful of chicken mixture. Heat the oil in a wok over high heat and fry the wrapped chicken for 5 minutes on each side or until cooked. Serve hot. Prior to eating, remove leaves. **Serves 4-6.**

CHICKEN WITH EGGPLANT
(Pad Makua Gai)

2 cups Japanese eggplant

5 tablespoons vegetable oil

4 cloves garlic, crushed

1 teaspoon salt

1 cup boneless chicken
  breast, thinly sliced

2 red chili peppers, thinly
  sliced

10 sweet basil leaves

Slice eggplant crosswise into slices 1/8-inch thick. In a wok, heat the oil over high heat and add the garlic, salt, eggplant and chicken. Stir-fry for 8 minutes. Add the red chili peppers and basil leaves. Stir well for 1 minute. Serve hot. **Serves 4-6.**

CHICKEN BREAST WITH CASHEW
(Pad Gai Met Mamuang Himapan)

4 tablespoons vegetable oil

3 cloves garlic, crushed

1 lb boneless chicken
  breast, thinly sliced

4 tablespoons oyster sauce

6 whole dried red chili
  peppers

10 green onions, cut into
  1-inch lengths

1 cup unsalted roasted
  cashew nuts

4 tablespoons fresh
  coriander leaves

In a wok, heat the oil over medium heat. Add the garlic and stir-fry until light brown. Add the chicken and oyster sauce. Cook for 8 minutes. Add the red chili peppers, green onions, and cashew nuts. Stir well and cook for 2 more minutes. Garnish with fresh coriander leaves. **Serves 4.**

AROMATIC FRIED CHICKEN
(Gai Tord)

2 chicken breasts

4 cloves garlic, crushed

1 teaspoon ground white pepper

4 tablespoons fish sauce (Nam Pla)

1 tablespoon fresh lime juice

4 tablespoons fresh coriander leaves, finely chopped

2 tablespoons cornstarch

2 cups vegetable oil for deep-frying

In a bowl, marinate the chicken breasts with garlic, white pepper, fish sauce, lime juice, and coriander leaves for 30 minutes in the refrigerator. Coat the chicken breasts with cornstarch on both sides and deep-fry in a wok over medium heat for about 3 minutes on each side or until golden brown. **Serves 2-4.**

CHAPTER EIGHT

RICE &
NOODLES

*coriander
or cilantro*

*green
onions*

*dried black
mushrooms*

CHAPTER EIGHT
RICE & NOODLES

THAI FRIED RICE, *(Khao Pad)* 99

PINEAPPLE VEGETARIAN FRIED RICE, *(Pad Khao Saparod)* 100

SPICY FRIED RICE, *(Khao Pad Prik)* 101

STIR-FRIED NOODLES, *(Pad Thai)* 102

CRISPY FRIED VERMICELLI, *(Mee Krob)* 103

STIR-FRIED VERMICELLI, *(Pad Wun Sen)* 104

shallots

THAI FRIED RICE
(Khao Pad)

4 tablespoons vegetable oil

2 eggs, beaten

1 yellow onion, finely chopped

3 cloves garlic, crushed

1 lb pork chops, finely cut into julienne strips

1/2 lb small shrimp, shelled and deveined

1 can crab meat (6 1/2 oz.)

1 teaspoon salt

1 teaspoon ground black pepper

2 tablespoons fish sauce (Nam Pla)

2 fresh hot red chilies, cut into julienne strips

2 tablespoons ketchup

4 cups cooked rice

1/2 cup green onions, chopped

4 tablespoons fresh coriander, chopped

Heat 2 tablespoons of oil in a wok, and stir-fry the eggs as you would scrambled eggs. Then set them aside. In the same wok, pour in the remaining oil and fry the onion and garlic until golden brown. Add the pork, shrimp, crab, salt, pepper, fish sauce, chilies, and ketchup. Stir-fry for 5 minutes. Add the stir-fried eggs and rice. Stir well for 2 minutes. On a plate, arrange the Thai fried rice and garnish with green onion and fresh coriander. **Serves 6.**

PINEAPPLE VEGETARIAN FRIED RICE
(Pad Khao Saparod)

4 tablespoons vegetable oil

1 yellow onion, finely chopped

3 cloves garlic, crushed

1 cup finely chopped carrots

1 cup finely chopped green beans

1 cup pineapple chunks

3 cups cooked rice

1 tablespoon ketchup

1 teaspoon salt

1 cucumber, thinly sliced

4 tablespoons green onion, chopped

4 tablespoons fresh coriander leaves

In a wok, heat the oil over medium heat and stir-fry the onion and garlic until golden brown. Add the carrots and green beans and stir-fry for 2 minutes. Add the pineapple, rice, ketchup, and salt. Mix well and stir-fry for 3 more minutes. Arrange the sliced cucumber around the serving platter. Pour the stir-fried rice in the center. Garnish with green onion and fresh coriander leaves. Serve hot. **Serves 4-6.**

SPICY FRIED RICE
(Khao Pad Prik)

4 tablespoons vegetable oil

2 eggs, beaten

1 red onion, finely chopped

1 fresh red chili, cut into julienne strips

1 tablespoon Red Curry Paste (See page 21.)

1 lb medium-sized prawns, shelled and deveined

3 cups cooked rice

1 teaspoon salt

1 teaspoon ground black pepper

2 tablespoons fish sauce (Nam Pla)

1 tablespoon light soy sauce

1 cup green onion, finely chopped

1/2 cup fresh coriander, chopped

1 tomato, cut into 6 wedges

1 cucumber, thinly sliced

1 lime, cut into 6 wedges

Heat 2 tablespoons of oil in a wok and stir-fry the eggs as you would for scrambled eggs. Set them aside. In the same wok, pour in the remaining oil and fry the onion, chili, curry paste, and prawns for 3 minutes. Then add the scrambled eggs, rice, salt, pepper, fish sauce, soy sauce, and green onion. Stir well for 2 minutes and serve hot. Garnish with fresh coriander, tomato wedges, cucumber slices, and lime wedges. **Serves 4-6.**

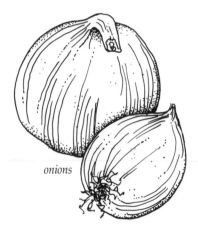

onions

STIR-FRIED NOODLES
(Pad Thai)

1 pkg. (16 oz.) flat rice stick noodles

4 tablespoons vegetable oil

4 cloves garlic, crushed

1 yellow onion, chopped

1 1/2 lbs pork loin, cut into julienne strips

1/2 cup dried shrimp, soaked in 1/2 cup of warm water for 5 minutes

2 fresh red chilies, cut into julienne strips

1 teaspoon white sugar

1/8 cup fish sauce (Nam Pla)

1 teaspoon salt

2 tablespoons lime juice

3 tablespoons ketchup

1 teaspoon ground black pepper

1 lb fresh bean sprouts, washed, drained

4 tablespoons green onion, chopped

4 tablespoons fresh coriander, chopped

4 tablespoons roasted peanuts, crushed

In a pot of boiling water, drop in the flat rice stick noodles for about 1 minute, stirring constantly to prevent noodles from sticking together. Remove from heat and drain in a colander. Rinse with cold water. Set aside. Heat the oil in a large wok and stir-fry the garlic and onion until golden brown. Add the pork, shrimp in water, and chilies. Stir-fry for 5 minutes and add the sugar, fish sauce, salt, lime juice, ketchup, black pepper, noodles, and bean sprouts. Stir well for 2 minutes. Transfer to a large serving platter and garnish with green onion, fresh coriander and peanuts. **Serves 6-8.**

CRISPY FRIED VERMICELLI
(Mee Krob)

4 tablespoons vegetable oil

4 cloves garlic, crushed

1 lb pork loin, cut into julienne strips

1 whole boneless chicken breast, skinned, cut into julienne strips

1 lb small raw prawns, shelled, deveined

6 dried black Chinese mushrooms, soaked in 1/4 cup of warm water for 10 minutes, (Save the water.), cut into julienne strips (Note: Discard hard ends from stems.)

1/2 cup string beans, diagonally sliced

2 tablespoons lime juice

4 tablespoons light soy sauce

4 tablespoons fish sauce (Nam Pla)

2 fresh hot red chilies, finely chopped

2 cups vegetable oil (for frying the rice vermicelli)

1 pkg. (8 oz.) rice vermicelli

4 tablespoons fresh coriander, chopped

Heat 4 tablespoons of oil in a wok and fry the garlic, pork, chicken and prawns for 5 minutes. Then add the black mushrooms and soaking water, string beans, lime juice, soy sauce, fish sauce, and chilies. Stir very well for 3 minutes. Set aside. In a separate wok, heat 2 cups of oil over high heat and fry rice vermicelli in handfuls. (Do not soak the vermicelli: use it straight from the package.) The oil should be very hot, so the vermicelli puffs and swells immediately. Test heat of oil with a little vermicelli first. Turn vermicelli and fry the other side. Lift out and drain on paper towels. In a big bowl, arrange the fried vermicelli with the other mixture of meat and vegetables. Garnish with fresh coriander. Serve immediately. **Serves 4-6.**

STIR-FRIED VERMICELLI
(Pad Wun Sen)

1 pkg. (8 oz.) rice vermicelli

4 tablespoons vegetable oil

1 yellow onion, chopped

3 cloves garlic, crushed

1 lb pork loin, thinly sliced

1/2 cup dried shrimp,
   soaked in 1/4 cup of
   warm water for 5 minutes

1 fresh hot red chili, thinly
   sliced

2 carrots, cut into julienne
   strips

1 teaspoon ground black
   pepper

4 tablespoons fish sauce
   (Nam Pla)

4 tablespoons green onion,
   chopped

4 tablespoons fresh
   coriander leaves,
   chopped

In a bowl with warm water, soak the rice vermicelli for 10 minutes and drain well. Set aside. In a wok, heat the oil over medium heat and stir-fry the onion and garlic until golden brown. Add the pork and shrimp in water and stir-fry for 5 minutes. Add the chili, carrots, pepper, and fish sauce and stir well for 2 minutes. Add the vermicelli and stir well for a minute. Arrange on a serving platter and garnish with green onion and fresh coriander leaves.
Serves 2-4.

CHAPTER NINE

DESSERTS

pandanus
leaves

coconut

CHAPTER NINE

DESSERTS

GLUTINOUS RICE AND MANGO, *(Khao Niew Mamuang)* **107**

BLACK RICE WITH COCONUT MILK, *(Khao Niew Dum Gathi)* **107**

CUSTARD IN PUMPKIN, *(Fak Thong Sung-Khaya)* **108**

STEWED BANANAS IN SYRUP, *(Glouy Boud Chee)* **108**

COCONUT CUSTARD, *(Kanom Mokang Muang Petch)* **109**

THAI WINTER SQUASH CUSTARD, *(Sang Kaya)* **109**

COCONUT ICE CREAM, *(Idem Gati)* **110**

MANGO ICE CREAM, *(Mamuang Idem)* **110**

THAI ICED COFFEE, *(Gafa Yen)* **111**

THAI ICED TEA , *(Cha Yen)* **111**

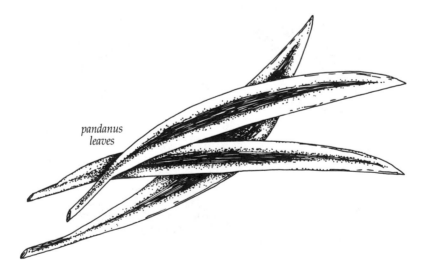

pandanus leaves

GLUTINOUS RICE AND MANGO
(Khao Niew Mamuang)

1 cup glutinous rice

1 can coconut milk
(14 fl. oz.)

1 cup white sugar

a pinch of salt

1 fresh or dried pandanus
leaf

2 fresh mangoes, peeled,
cut into small cubes

Soak the rice overnight in cold water, then cook it in a steamer for 30 minutes or until the rice is soft. In a saucepan, cook the coconut milk, sugar, salt and pandanus leaf over a low heat for 20 minutes. Let the rice and the coconut mixture cool. Discard the pandanus leaf. In individual serving dishes, scoop a tablespoon of rice and mango and pour the coconut milk mixture on top. **Serves 4-6.**

BLACK RICE WITH COCONUT MILK
(Khao Niew Dum Gathi)

2 cups black rice, washed,
soaked overnight and
drained

4 cups water

1 can coconut milk
(14 fl. oz.)

1 cup white sugar

a pinch of salt

1 fresh or dried pandanus
leaf

In a medium-sized uncovered pot, bring the rice and water to a boil over high heat for 3 minutes, stirring occasionally. Reduce the heat to low and simmer covered for 1 hour or until the rice is soft. Let the rice cool. In a saucepan, cook the coconut milk, sugar, salt and pandanus leaf over a low heat for 20 minutes. Discard the pandanus leaf. In individual serving dishes, scoop 2 tablespoons of black rice and pour the coconut mixture on top. Serve at room temperature. **Serves 4-6.**

CUSTARD IN PUMPKIN
(Fak Thong Sung-Khaya)

1 small pumpkin

3 eggs, well-beaten

1/2 cup brown sugar

a pinch of salt

1 can coconut milk
(14 fl. oz.)

Cut off the top of the pumpkin, remove the seeds and most of the soft pulp. In a bowl, mix the beaten eggs, brown sugar, salt, and coconut milk and stir until blended. Pour the mixture into the pumpkin, replace the top of the pumpkin and cook in a bamboo steamer until the custard is set, approximarely 40 minutes. **Serves 4-6.**

STEWED BANANAS IN SYRUP
(Glouy Boud Chee)

1 can coconut milk
(14 fl. oz.)

a pinch of salt

1/2 cup white sugar

1/2 cup water

2 pandanus leaves

6 ripe plantain bananas, peeled and halved crosswise

In a small bowl, mix coconut milk and salt. Set aside. In a large saucepan, bring sugar, pandanus leaves and water to a boil over high heat, stirring constantly. Add bananas and reduce heat to low. Cook uncovered for 10 minutes or until liquid is clear and bananas are tender. Discard the pandanus leaves. Pour the coconut milk over the bananas. Serve at room temperature. **Serves 6.**

Coconut Custard
(Kanom Mokang Muang Petch)

1 can coconut milk
(14 fl. oz.)

4 eggs, well-beaten

1/2 cup white sugar

1/4 cup evaporated milk

Combine coconut milk, eggs, sugar and evaporated milk. Pour into a pot and cook over medium heat for 10 minutes until it becomes a smooth sauce. Pour slowly into a 9 x 9 inch pan and bake about 30 minutes in preheated oven at 350 degrees. **Serves 4-6.**

Thai Winter Squash Custard
(Sang Kaya)

4 eggs

1/4 cup palm or brown
sugar

1/4 cup white sugar

1 can coconut milk
(14 fl. oz.)

a pinch of salt

1 cup winter squash,
peeled, thinly sliced

In a deep bowl, beat the eggs well. Add the brown and white sugar and stir until dissolved. Add the coconut milk, salt and squash and stir well. Pour mixture into a 9-by-9-inch baking pan. Cook in a bamboo steamer over high heat for 30 minutes or until the custard is set. **Serves 4-6.**

COCONUT ICE CREAM
(Idem Gati)

1 pint whipping cream

1 can coconut milk
(14 fl. oz.)

1/8 teaspoon salt

1 cup white sugar

1/2 cup peanuts, whole,
unsalted, roasted

1 can (20 oz.) palm seeds

In a large bowl, mix the whipping cream, coconut milk, salt and sugar. Put the mixture in an ice cream maker or place the mixture in a pan in the freezer and freeze until it is icy and almost set. Scrape it into a mixing bowl and beat it thoroughly with a wooden spoon, or at low speed with an electric mixer. Return it to the freezer and freeze until it is set. Serve the ice cream with peanuts and palm seeds. **Serves 4.**

MANGO ICE CREAM
(Mamuang Idem)

2 large ripe mangoes,
peeled, seeded

1 cup white sugar

1/8 teaspoon salt

1 pint whipping cream

2 tablespoons fresh orange
juice

1 large ripe mango, peeled,
seeded, thinly sliced

Blend in the blender the mangos, sugar, and salt. In a large bowl, mix the mango mixture with the whipping cream and orange juice. Put the mixture in an ice cream maker or place the mixture in a pan in the freezer and freeze until it is icy and almost set. Scrape it into a mixing bowl and beat it thoroughly with a wooden spoon, or at low speed with an electric mixer. Return it to the freezer and freeze until it is set. Serve the ice cream with thin slices of ripe mangos. **Serves 4.**

THAI ICED COFFEE
(Gafa Yen)

1/4 cup of ground coffee

4 cups of water

crushed ice

1 can of sweetened,
  condensed milk

In a 6 inch strainer, place a coffee filter. Put the coffee into the filter and place over a 2 quart pot. Bring the water to a boil and pour over the coffee. Stir the water continuously into the coffee filter. Let cool to lukewarm. Pour into tall glasses filled with ice. Add about 1 inch of condensed milk and stir. **Serves 4.**

THAI ICED TEA
(Cha Yen)

1 can of sweetened,
  condensed milk

1 can of evaporated milk

1/4 cup Thai tea leaves (red or black)

4 cups water

crushed ice

Combine the sweetened, condensed milk and the evaporated milk. Set aside. In a 6 inch strainer, place a coffee filter. Put the tea leaves in the filter and place in a 2 quart pan. Bring the water to a boil, then pour it onto the tea leaves. Stir thoroughly and let steep in the pan for two or three minutes. Remove strainer and discard the tea leaves. Allow tea to cool to lukewarm. Pour the tea into tall glasses filled with crushed ice. Add about 1 inch of the milk mixture and stir. **Serves 4.**

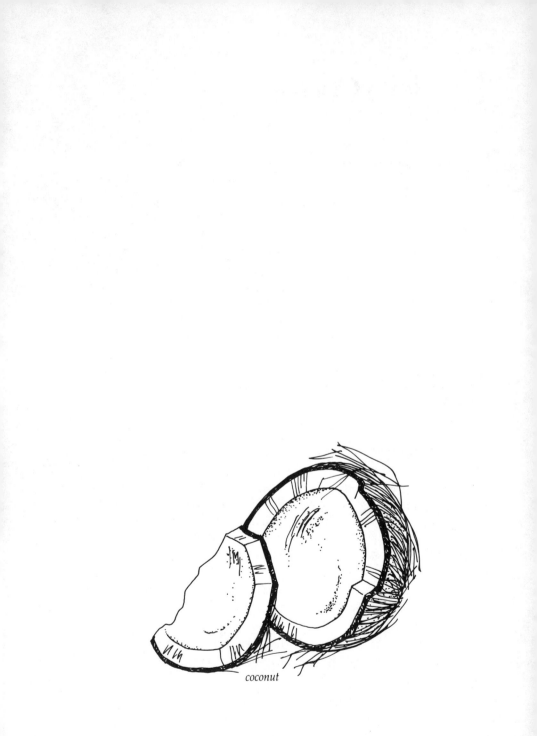

coconut

Wrapping Spring Rolls

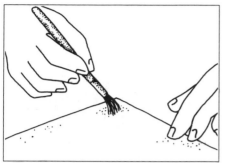

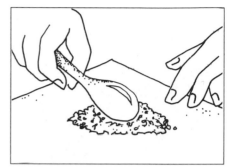

1. Place a wrapper with one corner toward you. Brush on a little egg yolk and water on each corner to seal the spring roll.

2. Put two tablespoons of the filling 1/3 of the way from the corner.

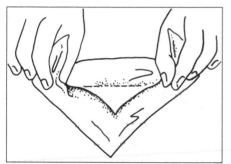

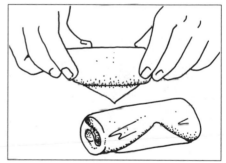

3. Fold the closest edge over the filling; then fold the right and left edges.

4. Roll up the spring roll. Make sure the final edge sticks to the body.

DEBONING CHICKEN WINGS

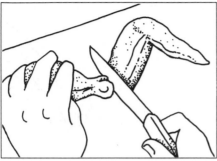

1. Separate the wing from the chicken.

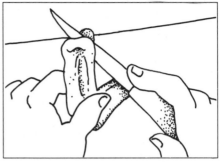

2. Carefully cut between the two bones at the joint to separate the two bones.

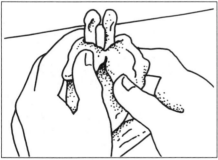

3. Slide the skin down the two bones, separating the meat from the bones.

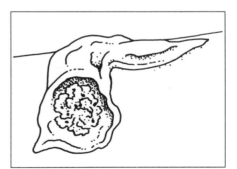

4. At the base of the bones, cut the tendon and remove the bones. Stuff the mixture into the wing pocket, leaving the pocket open.

Cleaning and Scoring Squid

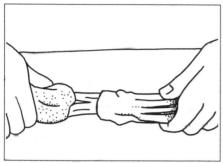

1. Pull the tentacles from the body of the squid. Intestines will also come out.

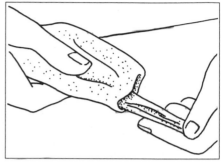

2. Pull out the quill from the body.

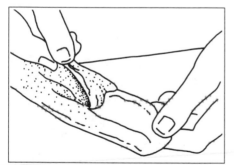

3. Peel off the outer skin. Rinse out the body. Cut the tentacles off at the head.

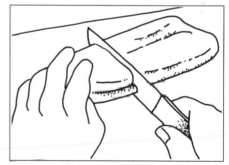

4. Cut to size, depending on recipe.

SHELLING AND DEVEINING SHRIMP

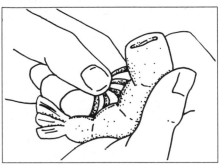

1. From the underside of the shrimp, remove the legs.

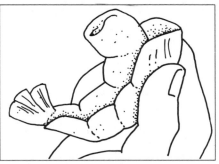

2. Roll back the shell from the underside, (remove or keep tail, as desidred).

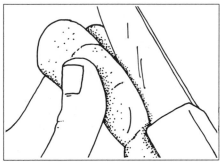

3. To devein, cut along the back (not completely through) and remove the vein.

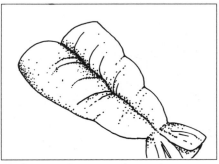

4. If butterflying is desired, cut deeper along the back and spread the halves open along the cut in the back.

Essential Ingredients

- Canned Coconut Milk
- Cardamom Pods
- Dried Chinese Black Mushrooms
- Dried Red Chilies or Dried Cayenne
- Fish Sauce
- Flat Rice Stick Noodles
- Fresh Coriander Leaves and Fresh Coriander Root
- Fresh Holy Basil or Fresh Sweet Basil
- Fresh Lime and Fresh Lime Juice
- Fresh Mint Leaves
- Fresh Tamarind Seed Pods or Tamarind Liquid
- Galangal (Laos Root) (Kha)
- Garlic
- Glutinous and Short Grain Rice
- Ginger
- Green Chili Peppers (Cayenne, Serrano, Jalapeno)
- Ground Black and White Pepper
- Ground Coriander

- Ground Cumin
- Kaffir Lime Leaves
- Kaffir Lime Rind or Lemon Rind
- Ketchup
- Lemon Grass
- Oyster Sauce
- Palm or Brown Sugar
- Pandanus Leaves
- Red Chili Peppers (Cayenne, Serrano, Jalapeno)
- Red Onion
- Rice Vinegar
- Roasted Peanuts
- Shrimp Sauce or Paste
- Soy Sauce
- Turmeric Powder

GLOSSARY

BAMBOO SHOOTS - A crisp, cream-colored, conical-shaped vegetable used frequently in all Asian cooking. It is much simpler to buy the canned variety which is readily available in all Asian stores and many Western supermarkets.

BASIL - A strong and pungent herb. There are various types, but two types are used most often in Thai cooking: Bai Kra Pow, (Holy basil), both purple and white, available in Asian markets, both fresh and dried; and Bai-horapa (Italian sweet basil), available fresh or dried in Asian and Western markets.

BEAN SPROUTS- The sprouts of the green mung bean. Fresh sprouts are found in Asian and Western markets.

BEAN CURD - Known as Tofu, made from soy beans and available in Asian and Western markets. Sold deep-fried in 4 oz. packages.

BLACK MUSHROOMS - Known as Chinese mushrooms. Sold dried; however, must be soaked in warm water for some time before using. The hard stems are discarded. Available in Asian and Western markets.

BLACK RICE - A dark purple, long grained, glutinous rice. Used for desserts mainly.

CARDAMOM - Grown mainly in India and Ceylon, the dried seed pods are either pale green or brown, according to variety. Sometimes they are bleached white. They are added, either whole or crushed, to rice dishes and spiced curries, such as masaman curry and others. Also used in sweets. When using ground cardamom, the seed pods are opened and discarded and only the small, black or brown seeds are ground. For the best flavor, grind them just before using or crush the seeds in a mortar.

CELLOPHANE NOODLES - Also known as "bean thread vermicelli", a firm transparent noodle made from mung beans. They are usually soaked in warm water for 5 minutes before use. They are also deep-fried straight from the packet, when used as a garnish.

CHILIES - Three varieties are used in this book: red and green cayenne, and green and red serrano and jalapeno from from Mexico. In Thailand there are many varieties, the very hot, small green chili are called Prik Khee Noo. Also dried chilies are quite often used whole or crushed.

CINNAMON - It is native to Sri Lanka (Ceylon). Use cinnamon sticks rather than the ground spice, which loses its flavor when stored too long. It is used in both sweet and savory dishes.

CLOVES - Cloves are the dried flower buds of a tropical evergreen tree native to Southeast Asia.

COCONUT MILK - Freshly grated coconut is used to make coconut milk by adding water, squeezing and straining. Where fresh coconuts are not available, the unsweetened canned coconut milk from Thailand is also excellent, convenient and available in Asian stores.

CORIANDER - One of the most essential ingredients in Thai cooking. The seeds, roots and leaves are all used and each has its own distinctive flavor. Also, fresh coriander is known as Chinese parsley or cilantro.

CUMIN - It is the most essential ingredient in the preparation of curry. It is available in seed form, or ground.

DRIED SHRIMP PASTE OR SAUCE - A pungent paste made from prawns, and used in many Southeast Asian recipes. It is sold in cans, jars or flat slabs and will keep indefinitely. Known as Kapi in Thailand and Traci in Indonesia.

FISH SAUCE - Called Nam Pla in Thailand, a thin, salty, brown sauce used in Southeast Asian cooking to bring out the flavor in food.

GALANGAL OR LAOS ROOT - It is delicate in flavor with brown skin and creamy white flesh. It is sold in powder form or as a dried root in Asian markets. Called Kha in Thailand.

GLUTINOUS RICE - A long-grained variety of rice known as sticky-rice. It is used frequently for rice desserts.

JAPANESE EGGPLANT - Four to five inches long, about two inches in diameter, this eggplant is very tasty and tender.

KAFFIR LIME OR FRAGRANT LIME - Called Makrood in Thai. The peel, juice and leaves are used in Malaysian, Indonesian and Thai cooking.

LEMON GRASS - An aromatic type of grass with a strong lemony fragrance, known as "serah", it grows with a small bulbous root. Grated lemon peel can be used as a poor substitute. An absolutely essential ingredient of Thai cooking.

MINT - There are many varieties, however, the common round-leafed mint (spearmint) is the one most often used in Thai cooking.

NUTMEG - Used in curries, sweets and cakes. For a strong flavor, grate finely just before using.

OYSTER SAUCE - Made from oysters cooked in salted water and soy sauce. Keeps well and adds a delicate flavor to meat and vegetable dishes.

PALM SEEDS - Transparent, walnut-sized seeds gotten from a green, segmented coconut. Used as a garnish for coconut ice cream dishes or eaten as a chilled fruit. Available only in cans in America.

PALM SUGAR - A strong-flavored, dark sugar made from the sap of coconut palms and Palmyrah palms. Dark brown sugar can be substituted.

PANDANUS LEAVES - These long, flat, green leaves are either crushed or boiled to yield their flavor and color. Always remove prior to serving, except when cooking Fried Chicken in Pandanus Leaves. Used as flavoring in rice, chicken, curries and sweets.

PLANTAIN BANANA - A flattish, squarish, stubby banana which remains greeny-yellow even when ripe. It is the best of all cooking bananas, especially for desserts.

RICE FLOUR - It is ground rice and can be bought at Asian stores and health food stores. It gives a crispier texture when used in batters or other mixtures.

RICE VERMICELLI - These noodles are very thin, white threads made from rice flour.

SOY BEAN PASTE - A condiment of salty taste made from soy beans.

TAMARIND - An acid-tasting fruit, shaped like a large broad bean with a brittle brown shell, inside of which are shiny dark seeds covered with brown flesh. It is sold dried in packets. Before using in a recipe, soak tamarind rind in warm water for 5 minutes or until soft. Then squeeze until it mixes with the water. Next, strain out the seeds and fibers. Tamarind liquid is used to add a distinctively sour taste and should only be used in small quantities.

TAPIOCA FLOUR - Ground cassava root used for desserts and as a thickening agent in cooking. Readily available in most Asian markets.

TOFU - Also known as Bean Curd, made from soy beans and available in Asian and Western Markets. Sold deep-fried in 4-oz. packages.

TURMERIC POWDER - Belonging to the ginger family, turmeric has an orange-yellow color and is used for satays and curries, as well as in many other dishes. 1 teaspoon of turmeric powder is equal to 1 slice (1/2 inch) of fresh turmeric root.

WATER CHESTNUTS - Usually canned, but occasionally found fresh, water chestnuts have a crunchy texture. When fresh, their brown skin must be peeled off with a sharp knife and discarded.

Markets for Thai Ingredients

California

Bangkok Market, Inc.
4757 Melrose Ave.
Los Angeles, CA 90029
Tel. (213) 662-9705

Bezjian's Grocery, Inc.
4725 Santa Monica Blvd.
Los Angeles, CA 90029
Tel. (213) 662-1503

Yeen Sing Chong Company
977 North Broadway
Los Angeles, CA 90012
Tel. (213) 626-9619

Connecticut

Bangkok Store
1932 Park St.
Hartford, CT 06106
Tel. (203) 236-7046

Georgia

Dekalb Farmers Market
3000 E Ponce de Leon Ave.
Decatur, GA 30030
Tel. (404) 377-6400

Illinois

Thailand Food Corp.
Thailand Plaza
4821 N Broadway St.
Chicago, IL 60640
Tel. (312) 728-1199

Thai Grocery Inc.
5014 N Broadway
Chicago, IL 60640
Tel. (312) 769-0800

Thai Oriental Grocery
5124 S. Kedzie
Chicago, IL 60632
Tel. (312) 436-7381

Maryland

Asian Food Inc.
2301 University Blvd. West
Wheaton, MD 20902
Tel. (301) 933-6071

Asian Food Market
615 S. Frederick Rd
Gaithersburg, MD 20877
Tel. (301) 948-1344

Maryland Cont.

Thai Market
902 Thayer Ave.
Silver Springs, MD 20912
Tel. (301) 495- 2779

New York

Aphrodisia Products, Inc.
282 Bleker St.
New York, NY 10014
Tel. (212) 989-6440

Bangkok Village Grocery Inc.
206 Thompson
New York, NY 10013
Tel. (212) 777-9272

Chinese-American Trading Co.
91 Mulberry St.
New York, NY 10013
Tel. (212) 267-5224

House of Spices
76-17 Broadway
Jackson Heights, Queens, NY 11373
Tel. (212) 476-1577

Poo Ping Corp.
81 A Bayard St.
New York, NY 10013
Tel. (212) 349-7662

Siam Grocery
790 9th Ave.
New York, NY 10019
Tel. (212) 245-4660

Oregon

Anzen Japanese Foods and Imports
736 Northeast Union Ave.
Portland, OR 97232
Tel. (503) 233-5111

Texas

Asian Grocery
9191 Forest Ln. # 3
Dallas, TX 75243
Tel. (214) 235-3038

Diho Market Texas Inc.
9280 Bellaire Blvd.
Houston, TX 77036
Tel.(713) 988-1881

Siam and Loaf Market
6929 Longpoint
Houston, TX 77055
Tel. (713) 681-0751

Washington

Asian Connection Store
409 Maynard S.
Seattle, WA 98144
Tel. (206) 587-6010

Beacon Market
2500 Beacon S.
Seattle, WA 98104
Tel. (206) 323-2050

House of Rice
4112 University Way NE.
Seattle, WA 98105
Tel. (206) 545-6956

Uwajimaya Inc.
6th S. & S.King
Seattle, WA 98104
Tel. (206) 624-6248

Viet Hoa Market
676 S. Jackson
Seattle, WA 98144
Tel. (206) 621-8499

Wa Sang Co.
663 S. King
Seattle, WA 98104
Tel. (206) 622-2032

Welcome Supermarket
1200 S. Jackson
Seattle, WA 98144
Tel. (206) 329-7044

INDEX

A

Appetizers
Deep-Fried Fish Cakes, 29
Galloping Horses, 25
Stuffed, Deep-Fried
Chicken Wings, 27
Stuffed Tofu with Ground
Pork, 26
Thai Satay, 30
Thai Spring Rolls, 28

B

(Stewed) Bananas in Syrup, 108
Bean Sprouts with Tomatoes, 58
(Stir-Fried) Bean Sprouts and
Tofu, 57
(String) Bean Salad, 48
Beverages
Thai Iced Coffee, 111
Thai Iced Tea, 111
Beef
Beef Curry with Eggplant, 85
Green Curry with Beef, 79
Orange Beef, 80
Panaeng Beef Curry, 84
Spicy Beef Soup, 39
Spicy Fried Ginger Beef, 81
Stir-Fried Beef with Basil, 83
Stir-Fried Beef with Chilies, 82
Thai Beef Salad, 46
Broccoli in Oyster Sauce, 58

C

Cabbage Salad, 50
Chicken
Aromatic Fried Chicken, 96
Chicken Breast with Cashew, 95
Chicken Curry, 88
Chicken in Coconut Soup, 33
Chicken Masaman Curry, 92
Chicken Rice Soup, 34
Chicken with Black
Mushrooms, 89
Chicken with Eggplant, 95
Deboning Chicken Wings, 114
Fried Chicken in Pandanus
Leaves, 94
Spicy Ground Chicken, 91
Stuffed Chicken Breasts, 90
Stuffed Deep-Fried Chicken
Wings, 27
Thai Barbecue Chicken, 93
(Stir-Fried) Clams with Basil, 66
Coconut Custard, 109
Coconut Ice Cream, 110
Coconut Pumpkin Soup, 40
(Stuffed) Crab Shells, 68
Crispy Fried Catfish, 73
Cucumber Salad, 51
Cucumber Sauce, 16
Curry
Chicken Curry, 88
Chicken Masaman Curry, 92
Green Curry Paste, 20

Green Curry with Beef, 79
Green Curry with Prawns, 70
Masaman Curry Paste, 19
Red Curry Paste, 21
Red Curry with Pork, 87
Yellow Curry Paste, 22
Custard in Pumpkin, 108

D

Deep-Fried
Crispy Fried Catfish, 73
Crispy Fried Snapper, 75
Deep-Fried Fish Cakes, 29
Fried Chicken in Pandanus
   Leaves, 94
Fried Fish with Tamarind, 76
Orange Beef, 80
Stuffed Chicken Breasts, 90
Stuffed Crab Shells, 68
Stuffed Deep-Fried Chicken
   Wings, 27
Stuffed Tofu in Ground Pork, 26
Thai Spring Rolls, 28
Desserts
Black Rice with Coconut
   Milk, 107
Coconut Custard, 109
Coconut Ice Cream, 110
Custard in Pumpkin, 108
Glutinous Rice and Mango, 107
Mango Ice Cream, 110
Stewed Bananas in Syrup, 108

Thai Winter Squash Custard, 109

E

Eggplant
Beef Curry with Eggplant, 85
Chicken with Eggplant, 95

F

Fish
Crispy Fried Catfish, 73
Crispy Fried Snapper, 75
Deep-Fried Fish Cakes, 29
Fish with Red Sauce, 74
Fried Fish with Tamarind, 76
Hot and Sour Seafood Soup, 37
Sweet and Sour Fish Sauce, 17
Sweet and Sour Fish Soup, 38

G

Galloping Horses, 25
Glutinous Rice and Mango, 107
Green Curry Paste, 20
Green Papaya Salad, 47
Green Curry with Beef, 79
Green Curry with Prawns, 70
Ground Toasted Rice, 18

H

Hot and Sour Prawn Soup, 36

Hot and Sour Seafood Soup, 37
Hot and Sour Stir-Fried
  Vegetables, 55

I

Ice Cream
  Coconut Ice Cream, 110
  Mango Ice Cream, 110

M

Mango
  Glutinous Rice and Mango, 107
  Ice Cream, 110
  (Chicken) Masaman Curry, 92
  Masaman Curry Paste, 19
  Mixed Vegetable Salad, 49
  (Spicy Steamed) Mussels, 65

N

Noodles
  Crispy Fried Vermicelli, 103
  Stir-Fried Noodles
    (Pad Thai), 102
  Stir-Fried Vermicelli, 104

O

Orange Beef, 80

P

(Green) Papaya Salad, 47
Pastes
  Green Curry Paste, 20
  Masaman Curry Paste, 19
  Red Curry Paste, 21
  Yellow Curry Paste, 22
Peanut Sauce
  Satay Peanut Sauce, 15
  Spinach with Peanut Sauce, 61
Pineapple Vegetarian Fried
  Rice, 100
Pork
  Pork Balls and Vegetables, 86
  Red Curry with Pork, 87
  Stuffed Tofu with Ground
    Pork, 26
  Thai Satay, 30
Prawns
  Curried Prawn Soup, 35
  Hot and Sour Prawn Soup, 36
  Spicy Prawn Salad, 43
  Shrimp with Garlic, 72
Pumpkin
  Coconut Pumpkin Soup, 40
  Custard in Pumpkin, 108

R

Red
  Fish with Red Sauce, 74
  Red Chili Sauce, 15

Red Curry Paste, 21
Red Curry with Pork, 87
Rice
 Black Rice with Coconut
  Milk, 107
 Chicken Rice Soup, 34
 Glutinous Rice with Mango, 107
 Ground Toasted Rice, 18
 Pineapple Vegetarian
  Fried Rice, 100
 Spicy Fried Rice, 101
 Thai Fried Rice, 99

S

Salad
 Cabbage Salad, 50
 Cucumber Salad, 51
 Dried Shrimp Salad, 44
 Green Papaya Salad, 47
 Mixed Fruit Salad, 52
 Mixed Vegetable Salad, 49
 Spicy Prawn Salad, 43
 String Bean Salad, 48
 Thai Beef Salad, 46
 Thai Squid Salad, 45
(Thai) Satay, 30
Sauces
 Chili Sauce with Tamarind, 18
 Cucumber Sauce, 16
 Plum Sauce, 16
 Red Chili Sauce, 15
 Satay Peanut Sauce, 15
 Sweet and Sour Fish Sauce, 17

Sweet and Sour Sauce, 17
Seafood
 Cleaning and Scoring
  Squid, 115
 Crispy Fried Catfish, 73
 Crispy Fried Snapper, 75
 Curried Prawn Soup, 35
 Deep-Fried Fish Cakes, 29
 Dried Shrimp Salad, 44
 Fish with Red Sauce, 74
 Fried Fish with Tamarind, 76
 Fried Squid with Hot Sauce, 67
 Green Curry with Prawns, 70
 Hot and Sour Prawn Soup, 36
 Hot and Sour Seafood
  Soup, 37
 Sauted Shrimp with Lemon
  Grass, 71
 Shelling and Deveining
  Shrimp, 116
 Shrimp with Garlic, 72
 Spicy Prawn Salad, 43
 Spicy Steamed Mussels, 65
 Stir-Fried Clams with Basil, 66
 Stuffed Crab Shells, 68
 Sweet and Sour Fish Soup, 38
 Sweet and Sour Shrimp, 69
 Thai Squid Salad, 45
Soup
 Chicken in Coconut Soup, 33
 Chicken Rice Soup, 34
 Coconut Pumpkin Soup, 40
 Curried Prawn Soup, 35
 Hot and Sour Prawn Soup, 36

Hot and Sour Seafood Soup, 37
Spicy Beef Soup, 39
Sweet and Sour Fish Soup, 38
Spicy Fried Ginger Beef, 81
Spicy Fried Rice, 101
Spicy Ground Chicken, 91
Spinach with Peanut Sauce, 61
(Thai) Spring Rolls, 28
Stewed Bananas in Syrup, 108
Stir-Fried
　Fried Squid with Hot Sauce, 67
　Hot and Sour Stir-Fried
　　Vegetables, 55
　Stir-Fried Bean Sprouts
　　and Tofu, 57
　Stir-Fried Beef with Basil, 83
　Stir-Fried Beef with Chilies, 82
　Stir-Fried Clams with Basil, 66
　Stir-Fried Mixed Vegetables, 60
　Stir-Fried Noodles (Pad
　　Thai), 102
　Stir-Fried Spinach, 56
　Stir-Fried Vermicelli, 104
　Tofu with Mixed Vegetables, 59
Stuffed Chicken Breasts, 90
Stuffed Crab Shells, 68
Stuffed Deep-Fried Chicken
　Wings, 27
Stuffed Tofu with Ground
　Pork, 26
Stuffed Zucchini, 62

T

Tamarind
　Chili Sauce with Tamarind, 18
　Fried Fish with Tamarind, 76
Tofu
　Stuffed Tofu with Ground
　　Pork, 26
　Tofu with Mixed Vegetables, 59

V

Vegetables
　Hot and Sour Stir-Fried
　　Vegetables, 55
　Mixed Vegetable Salad, 49
　Pork Balls and Vegetables, 86
　Stir-Fried Mixed Vegetables, 60
　Stuffed Zucchini, 62
　Tofu with Mixed Vegetables, 59
(Pineapple) Vegetarian Fried
　Rice, 100
(Crispy Fried) Vermicelli, 103

W

(Deboning Chicken) Wings, 114
(Thai) Winter Squash Custard, 109
Wrapping Spring Rolls, 113

Y

Yellow Curry Paste, 22